James Beard Award winners Jody Williams and Rita Sodi's restaurant, Via Carota ("New York's most perfect restaurant"—*The New Yorker*), is legendary for the wonderful Italian fare, warm atmosphere, and homey hospitality that attract chefs and celebrities from around the world. Emphasizing vegetables and seasonal cooking, the dishes that come out of their kitchen are astonishing in their simplicity yet dazzling in their elegance.

In *Via Carota: A Celebration of Seasonal Cooking from the Beloved Greenwich Village Restaurant,* they share the secrets to cooking Via Carota's traditional (but not too traditional) cuisine at home. Here are more than 140 recipes, including Meyer Lemon Risotto, Roasted Carrots with Spiced Yogurt and Pistachios, Tuscan Onion Soup, Potato Gnocchi, Sweet Ricotta Cake, and, of course, the restaurant's signature Insalata Verde.

These are dishes that celebrate the bounty of every time of year, highlighting the very best uses for the most delicious seasonal produce, from spring peas to summer squashes, autumnal legumes to winter citrus. A beautiful, deeply personal cookbook, *Via Carota* gives you everything you need to create impossibly flavorful, vegetable-centric Italian dishes in your own kitchen.

VIA CAROTA

51 GROVE STREET

N . Y . C

LIBRARY OF CONGRESS CATALOGING-IN-PUBLICATION DATA
Names: Williams, Jody, [date] author. | Sodi, Rita, author.
Title: Via Carota : a celebration of seasonal cooking from the beloved
Greenwich Village restaurant / Jody Williams and Rita Sodi with
Anna Kovel; photographs by Gentl & Hyers.
Description: New York: Alfred A. Knopf, 2022. | Includes index. |
Identifiers: LCCN 2021048956 (print) | LCCN 2021048957 (ebook) |
ISBN 9780525658573 (hardcover) | ISBN 9780525658580 (ebook)
Subjects: LCSH: Cooking (Vegetables) | Cooking, Italian. |
Via Carota (Restaurant) | LCGFT: Cookbooks. | Cookbooks.
Classification: LCC TX801 .W5155 2022 (print) | LCC TX801 (ebook) |
DDC 641.6/5—dc23/eng/20211020
LC record available at https://lccn.loc.gov/2021048956
LC ebook record available at https://lccn.loc.gov/2021048957

Some of the recipes in this book include raw eggs, meat, or fish.
When these foods are consumed raw, there is always the risk that
bacteria, which is killed by proper cooking, may be present. For this
reason, when serving these foods raw, always buy certified salmonella-
free eggs and the freshest meat and fish available from a reliable grocer,
and store them in the refrigerator until they are served. Because of
the health risks associated with the consumption of bacteria that
can be present in raw eggs, meat, and fish, these foods should not be
consumed by infants, small children, pregnant women, the elderly,
or any persons who may be immunocompromised. The author and
publisher expressly disclaim responsibility for any adverse effects that
may result from the use or application of the recipes and information
contained in this book.

Jacket photograph by Gentl & Hyers
Jacket design by John Gall

Manufactured in China
First Edition

Via Carota

A CELEBRATION OF SEASONAL COOKING FROM THE
BELOVED GREENWICH VILLAGE RESTAURANT

Jody Williams & Rita Sodi

WITH ANNA KOVEL

PHOTOGRAPHS BY GENTL & HYERS

ALFRED A. KNOPF

NEW YORK

2022

Forza!

Contents

2 · SUMMER

4 · APERITIVI

SALATINI

LITTLE SANDWICHES

5 · AUTUMN

MUSHROOMS

SQUASH

CABBAGES

LEEKS AND ONIONS

6 · WINTER

Introduction

MEETING ON CHRISTOPHER STREET

The first time I met Rita Sodi was in the spring of 2008. Her restaurant, I Sodi, had been open for a month or two, and I was lucky enough to find myself seated at the bar for a late solo dinner. I ordered her baccelli di fava and a risotto di asparagi from a small, handwritten menu. Twelve seats away was the chef and owner herself, enjoying a plate of carciofi fritti and a negroni. Little did I know that one day we would marry and work side by side in our neighborhood restaurants. Rita, as I would later learn, arrived in New York City in 2006 with a mission to share the food she grew up eating in Barberino di Mugello, near Florence, Italy. She found a spot on Christopher Street in New York's Greenwich Village and at the age of forty-five began a chaotic adventure as a restaurateur and chef. At that time, Christopher Street was a delight of gay bars (and a gay pet store!), sex shops, pizza by the slice, and nail salons. Two years later, I Sodi would open its doors as a thirty-seat ristorante Toscana, purposefully unadorned, the interior and furnishings made from an old American barn and Carrara marble, and featuring simple Florentine dishes complemented with a list of well-stirred negronis. I ate at I Sodi at least five more times before I had the courage to introduce myself. I finally decided to drop by one afternoon with a couple of pints of perfectly ripe Tristar strawberries from the Union Square Greenmarket. Rita approved—at least of the strawberries. I got to know her by hanging out with her in her kitchen in the afternoons. I was struck by how peaceful it was, the methodical pace of peeling asparagus, the quietness broken only by the rhythm of knives mincing mountains of onions, carrots, and celery, and then there was the sweet aroma of the sugo di carne slowly cooking away. All of which brought me right back to the days I spent learning to cook in a celebrated café in Reggio Emilia, a small town in northern Italy's Emilia-Romagna region. Three years there and three years in Rome, all with the hope of mastering the basics of Italian cooking—something Rita, an instinctive cook, seemed to have learned at birth. We had so much in common for two completely different people.

By summer, our lives were entwined with the ups and downs of caring for our restaurants and an occasional respite at Rita's home on Via del Carota outside of Florence. We were naive but compelled to keep going—and we survived the painful early days of uncertainty, when our restaurants were new (mine, Buvette, opened in early 2011), and the later, bruisingly busy days together as we expanded and joined forces. I still stop by often at I Sodi to peek into the pots and taste the sugo de carne, while around the corner on Grove Street, Via Carota, the restaurant we opened together, has grown with each season.   **JODY**

BUILDING ON GROVE STREET

Bagno a Ripoli rises in the southeast of Florence. I lived there, on Via del Carota, for fifteen years while I worked as a producer for fashion houses before moving to New York City. My home was a restored seventeenth-century stone villa, with gated gardens, centennial olive groves, and a view of the Fiorentine hills and a sliver of Brunelleschi's fifteenth-century cupola. The kitchen, my favorite part of the house, had a wood-burning hearth to cook in and a ten-foot chestnut table surrounded with English chapel chairs. Our restaurant Via Carota in New York City is inspired by the many moments Jody and I spent at this table and the meals we cooked together there.

Jody jokes that we opened Via Carota on Grove Street so we could actually see each other. I was struggling the first years, working long days and nights at I Sodi—cooking on the line, opening the restaurant in the mornings, and closing it every night. I was learning by trial and error, trying desperately to figure out this new restaurant-cooking thing. Jody was cooking around the corner on Grove Street at Buvette, her tiny French *gastrothèque* that never seemed to shut. It was all hard work, and her jest was not far from the truth.

We had less and less time to spend in Italy. Our home on Via del Carota was now left to caretakers and gardeners. So, while Jody was away in Paris opening the Buvette in South Pigalle, we agreed to sell the home in Italy and sign a lease on a shuttered Thai restaurant down the block from both of our Greenwich Village restaurants. We did not know what to expect of our collaboration. We had no name or specific plans—we only had our time in Italy. We knew we wanted to recreate our experience there, the place we loved most with the food we relished most. If we were lucky, it could be a place full of life where people would feel welcomed and nourished.   **RITA**

As much as we want to remember these beginnings, we also knew Via Carota would forge new paths. For us, that meant holding on to certain culinary traditions, while taking risks and creating our own. Jody is more experimental, building on years of experience in pursuit of distinct classic dishes. (To this day, many of her trademark recipes, dating back to the mid-1990s, remain staples at the New York City restaurants where she first developed them.) Rita is a purist. She sticks to tradition, and she cooks instinctively. The food we create at Via Carota is the offspring of our different approaches and personalities.

For Via Carota, we imagined a world where we could be free from the formality of traditional restaurant dining. We rarely order what others consider a main course when we eat out. We prefer a table full of vegetables. Not that we don't enjoy a beautiful grilled fish or few slices of steak; it's just that we always want more vegetables, more tastes and textures. We crave antipasti, salads, beans, and vegetables. They are the triumphs of the season, each emphasizing one ingredient. Importantly, they are also for sharing. Spooning some thinly sliced artichokes or borlotti beans with farro onto your tablemate's plate and then spooning the same onto your own is an intimate experience.

We want Via Carota to transport you to another place and time, where we have breathed in the rustic beauty and uncomplicated flavors. When you sit down in the restaurant's birch chapel chairs at the wooden tables, it's visceral. Some of these same chairs traveled from our home in Italy to our home in the West Village. We reclaimed decades-old wood from gymnasium floors and commissioned the craftsman Warren Muller to create his unique lighting throughout, one from vintage milk bottles. All of it is to complement and enhance your experience at Via Carota.

And over time, people have made Via Carota their own, a neighborhood spot where they can share a pile of fritti and a spritz, or warm up with a piping hot cacio e pepe lasagna. People come to our place because there is nothing dictated, you can eat how you want to eat here. Routinely, our guests ask us: Can we have the recipe? How did you make that?

Hence, we decided to write a cookbook, so that both regulars and those who have never had a chance to visit the restaurant can prepare some of these dishes at home.

Is *The Via Carota Cookbook* a vegetarian cookbook? Maybe a better description is "vegetable forward." As at our restaurant, where our guests can choose from an abundance of seasonal fruits and vegetables—asparagus, artichokes, beans, beets, carrots, lettuces, melons, plums, and tomatoes—we are providing many notes and recipes here about some of our favorite vegetables and fruits that will fulfill you and fill your table throughout the year, from spring and summer to autumn and winter. They can be served solo or with pasta. Many dishes are an ideal companion to marinated chicken or roasted pork. There are also recipes for a slow-roasted lamb and a mixed seafood grill.

Use this book to create your own meals around the produce available to you, to eat how you want to eat. The vegetable-centered approach is more important now than ever. We believe it's good for us and for the planet. We're adapting all the time, and we encourage you to do the same. While we often talk about breaking with tradition in our cooking, eating a vegetable-focused diet is, in fact, traditional.

Via Carota food is simple. The ingredients are at its core. Some of these recipes require more understanding and work, while others you'll commit to memory after a few times. And as every seasoned cook knows, you have to taste as you go, using all your senses. We hope you will explore and experiment and play with this cookbook, and that you will make our recipes your recipes.

Cooking with This Book

USING ALL YOUR SENSES

Throughout the book, we give the amounts, times, and temperatures that are needed for each recipe, but every stove has different burners, every skillet is a different weight, and the ingredients in your kitchen will not necessarily be the same twice, depending on the time of year and where you buy your herbs, vegetables, and fruits. Every cook has a different palate; we can tell you how we like our vinaigrette, but you may want fewer shallots, or more vinegar. Your olive oil might be fruitier than ours; maybe you'll want to use more lemon than we say. And, for another example, only you can make the call on whether you need one tablespoon of oil or two to coat your pan for cooking your greens.

Go into the kitchen with a curious mind. Learn as you go, make the adjustments that you need to make, and if there is an ingredient you don't like or don't have in your cabinet, consider leaving it out or making a substitution. We have arrived at this place as cooks by paying attention to what we like and what we don't like, to the sounds, tastes, and smells of what's cooking in our kitchens. Being flexible is the most important tool. Every day in the kitchen is a learning experience, and, just like in life, the more you have to think on your feet the more interesting it becomes.

We won't tell you how to shop, but this is what makes sense to us: see what's freshest, when possible, before you decide what to cook. If you shop at local markets and buy what's grown or produced close to home, freshness is a given.

Unless we specify otherwise:

- Olive oil is extra-virgin (see page xxiii on olive oil).
- Oil for deep frying is a 50/50 blend of extra-virgin olive oil and a neutral-flavored oil with a high smoke point, such as safflower oil.
- Buy the best salt you can. We prefer sea salt, for its minerals and texture.
- Pepper is Tellicherry and always freshly ground.
- Sugar is granulated.
- Butter is unsalted.
- Flour is unbleached.
- Citrus is unwaxed, and preferably organic, when using the zest.
- Pecorino Romano and Parmigiano Reggiano are freshly grated.

TOOLS AND TECHNIQUES

We are not kitchen technicians. We leave the produce we serve in its natural state and use a light touch. But sometimes, picking the proper tool for the job can make your work as a cook easier.

Tools

- **KNIVES AND SHARPENING STONE** We like sharp knives. In our restaurant kitchens and at home, we use Japanese-made knives with thin, Swedish steel blades, and we sharpen them by hand on a sharpening stone.
- **MANDOLINE** Slice radishes, fennel, and other firm vegetables paper thin. The light Japanese mandolines are portable. The stainless steel French mandolines are workhorses—our cooks use them to julienne zucchini for fritti.
- **VEGETABLE PEELER** There are many models, all with the same purpose—peeling carrots, potatoes, asparagus, and even artichoke bottoms. A peeler also comes in handy for shaving parmigiano.
- **MICROPLANE ZESTER** These small, fine-toothed graters are sharp and efficient—they're good for grating citrus zest, nutmeg, and cloves of garlic. We occasionally use them for grating parmigiano over a finished dish.

- **BOX GRATER** We use different sizes of the grater for different reasons, shaving carrots on the thin side for a salad, and cheese on the medium side, while Rita prefers the thicker shavings of parmigiano for her pasta.
- **SPIDER** With its loosely knitted wire basket, the spider is the best tool for frying because it doesn't drag hot oil from the pan the way a slotted spoon does. It is also ideal for lifting blanched vegetables and cooked pasta from pots of boiling water. The bamboo-handled version is inexpensive and widely available.
- **BENCH SCRAPER** A baker's tool, this is a rectangular, flat blade (not sharp) with a handle that's easy to grip. We use it to work with pasta frolla, a sweet pastry dough, and our gnocchi. It's also the best way to scrape clean a floury work surface.
- **PASTA MACHINE** We like to use the manual Imperia pasta machine with optional attachments.
- **ROLLING PIN** Get a good rolling pin that you like, ideally an Italian- or French-style straight rolling pin, with knob handles or without.
- **PASTRY WHEEL** We collect unique pasta tools from Bologna to Sardinia, but a fluted-edged wheel for trimming tortelli and cutting lattice strips is all you really need.
- **WOODEN PASTRY BOARD** If you are an avid pasta maker and bread baker we recommend a reversible board, approximately 30 x 20 inches with a front lip to grab the counter and a back lip to keep the flour from spilling over.

Ingredients

These are a few ingredients we use consistently for seasoning and finishing the dishes at Via Carota. Some are a bit costly but worth every penny.

EXTRA-VIRGIN OLIVE OIL

Good olive oil is the cornerstone of our kitchen and, therefore, of the recipes in this book. Choose extra-virgin, cold pressed. Note that no bottle is the same. Each olive oil will likely taste different due to the growing and harvesting conditions, packaging, and basic care of the product. Keep your most flavorful oil for salads and drizzling over finished dishes. If you are heating or frying with extra-virgin olive oil, use one that is affordable enough that you can buy it in a large bottle.

VINEGAR AND CHEESE

- Aged sherry vinegar is mellow enough to be our all-purpose vinegar.
- Aceto balsamico tradizionale, from Modena or Reggio Emilia. Just a few drops for a finishing touch.
- Parmigiano Reggiano, no imitators.
- Pecorino Romano, imported from Italy.

SALT

A flaky sea salt is what we use for finishing many of our dishes before they go to the table. We also keep coarse sea salt for salting water when we are cooking pasta or vegetables or making brines. For seasoning when we are cooking, kosher salt is more consistent due to its texture.

WATER

Water is an ingredient. We add a teaspoon or two to our vinaigrettes and dressings; it calms acidity down for the palate. We also use it for taking the burning bite out of shallots and raw onions; we rinse them under cold water or soak them in a bowl of water before using them in salads and dressings.

We use water at varying temperatures to wash our lettuces and herbs. Our greens get washed twice: once in lukewarm water to get rid of any soil that clings to the ribs and leaves, and once in cold water to invigorate them.

Water is also a tool. Before deep-frying zucchini and frutti di mare, or grilling mussels, we soak them in ice-cold water long enough to chill them thoroughly, about 30 minutes. Potatoes are soaked for 2 hours before frying to remove some of their starch.

A cold bath is also a good way to revive soft herbs (such as parsley, mint, basil, or cilantro). We soak herbs in a small bowl of ice water for a few minutes before using them to garnish a dish.

Via
Carota

I

Spring

Days start before dawn at Via Carota in the spring, and it's a pleasure to be outside in the brisk air, sweeping the sidewalk outside our restaurant. Grove Street goes one way, starting west of the restaurant near the Hudson River. It's so quiet at that end of the street that we can hear the midday laughter of the kids from the school nearby. On the other side of Via Carota is Seventh Avenue South, a main artery where taxis and cyclists rush by and the subway churns out foot traffic. Before leaves begin to appear on the trees, spring shows itself in new asparagus shoots, fava beans in fuzzy little pods, and foraged finds like nettles. We crave nourishment: raw vegetables, eggs, and big bowls of cooked greens. Small artichokes are shaved and served raw or grilled; leafy green vegetables are cooked slowly in olive oil. We seek to cook with little interference.

FAVAS

· · · · · · · · · · · · · ·

Eating the year's first fava beans marks the beginning of spring for us. We sit with a pile of favas on our narrow wooden table and talk over mounds of paperwork and other minutiae, peeling fava beans mindlessly and nibbling them with fresh pecorino. We grab the moment while we can.

JODY *&* RITA

Baccelli e Pecorino

YOUNG FAVAS, RADISHES, AND FRESH PECORINO

Baccelli, or fava in their pods, are shucked just before serving. Eat fava beans raw when they're very small and tender.

SERVES FOUR

2 spring onions

1¾ cups/240 grams blanched, peeled fava beans

7 fresh mint leaves

5 fresh basil leaves

5 tablespoons/70 ml extra-virgin olive oil

1 tablespoon/15 grams lemon juice

piece of young pecorino Romano cheese, about 4 ounces/ 120 grams

10 small radishes, very thinly sliced

salt

pepper

Thinly slice the spring onions and soak in cold water for a minute or two. Drain in a fine-mesh sieve and shake off the excess water. Toss the onion slices with the fava beans in a bowl. Tear the mint and basil into large pieces, leaving the smaller leaves whole.

Add the olive oil and lemon juice to the bowl and toss lightly to coat the spring onions and fava beans. Crumble the cheese and toss with the radishes and herbs into the salad. Season with salt and pepper, and drizzle with remaining dressing.

PECORINO ROMANO

There are many types of pecorino in Italy—almost every region and town make sheep's milk cheese their own way. For me, the best one is a young Tuscan pecorino (aged for thirty days if you can find it, or up to sixty days). It's mild. If you like cheese, you can eat it more or less with anything—favas, salami, sliced pears, or honey. (Pecorino with honey or pears are among my favorite combinations.)

When Jody and I use an aged pecorino, we create a rough texture by digging into the cheese with a fork or the tip of a paring knife, or even crumbling it with our hands, to break off pebble-sized pieces of varying sizes. **RITA**

HOW TO CHOOSE, COOK, AND PEEL FAVAS

Fresh fava pods will have a slight shine and, if you're lucky, even some leaves attached. Choose the smallest and greenest ones from the pile; avoid very large, lumpy pods—the large, yellowed fava beans inside will be starchy. Blackened scratches on the pods are often unavoidable and don't affect the beans inside. When buying, estimate that 1 pound/454 grams will yield about ¾ cup/100 grams of shelled favas.

Keep favas in their pods until you're ready to use them. Inside the pod, each fava bean is wrapped in a tight and chewy skin. Peel it off to find the little bean inside. This is fiddly work, but we think it's worth it for the sublimely tender bean inside each skin. Finding young favas you can eat raw is rare. However, if you do, they are so tender you don't need to take off the outer skin, nor do you need to blanch them. We blanch the beans to make it easier to take off the skin—it's not to cook the beans.

To blanch, drop shucked favas into a saucepan of boiling water for less than one minute. Cool on a plate before peeling off the outer skin by tearing the top. Pop out the bright green bean.

Insalata di Fave

FAVAS, ESCAROLE, AND MINT

This salad is one of our spring staples. We add leaves of butter lettuce and favas to crisp escarole to temper its bitterness.

SERVES TWO

1 tablespoon/15 ml lemon juice

1 small garlic clove, finely grated

salt

chili flakes, optional

2 teaspoons water

3 tablespoons/45 ml extra-virgin
  olive oil

3 large handfuls pale, inner leaves
  of escarole (from 2 heads)

2 large handfuls butter lettuce,
  such as Bibb or Boston (from
  1 head)

12 leaves fresh mint or basil,
  or both

¾ cup/100 grams blanched,
  peeled favas (see instructions
  on page 6)

¼ cup/25 grams finely grated
  pecorino Romano + more for
  serving

Stir the lemon juice and garlic together in a small bowl, and add a large pinch of salt. Add a small pinch of chili flakes, if desired. Stir in the water and then pour the olive oil into the bowl in a slow stream, whisking while you pour.

Toss the escarole and butter lettuce leaves together in a large bowl. Stack the herb leaves on top of each other in an orderly way. Roll them up and draw your knife across them to make fine shreds. Toss the herbs and the favas into the bowl. Pour in the dressing, tossing with your hands to coat each leaf. Add pecorino and toss again. Pile the salad onto plates and sprinkle with more pecorino.

Scafata

BRAISED FAVAS, PEAS, AND ESCAROLE

This medley of spring vegetables varies slightly each time we make it. Sometimes we put asparagus in our scafata, sometimes not. Sometimes artichokes, sometimes not. Other options are ramps, green garlic, or fiddleheads. Cook everything gently in water with olive oil until they become a soft, muted green.

SERVES FOUR

1 pound/454 grams baby or
    medium artichokes (4–6)
½ head of escarole (about 5 cups
    of leaves)
extra-virgin olive oil
2 large garlic cloves, thinly sliced
1 whole dried chili, or about
    ¼ teaspoon chili flakes
about ¼ cup/60 ml water
1 spring onion, sliced into thick
    rings
salt
½ cup/70 grams blanched, peeled
    fava beans (see instructions on
    page 6)
1 cup/130 grams shelled green peas
    (from about 1 pound/454 grams
    peas in their pods)
handful fresh basil leaves, torn

Trim the artichokes (see page 16 for trimming instructions—sometimes baby artichokes haven't developed a fuzzy choke, but if they do have some choke, then scoop it out). Slice the artichokes into thin wedges. Wash the escarole in two changes of cool water, and drain in a colander, shaking off the excess water. Slice the leaves into large pieces.

Pour a generous amount of olive oil (about ¼ cup/60 ml) into a medium saucepan, add the artichokes, garlic, chili, and water and bring to a simmer over medium heat. Cover the pot and cook until the artichokes are barely tender when pierced with a fork, about 5 minutes.

Raise the heat to medium high and stir in the spring onions and escarole with a pinch of salt. Toss the escarole to wilt, and cook until the artichokes are completely tender, about 5 minutes more. Stir in the fava beans and peas and cover the pot, cooking until the peas are tender, 3 to 4 minutes. Remove from the heat and stir in the basil. Season with salt as needed. Finish with a drizzle of olive oil.

BE PREPARED

Jody learned to cook in many different kitchens, from California to New York, to Japan and Italy, each place unique and challenging. When she was about nine years old, she began cooking on a hibachi, a small Japanese grill balanced on two bricks in her backyard. She collected recipes out of *Sunset*, the essential California cooking magazine. Her mother welcomed the help and praised her self-sufficiency. Jody learned at a young age that the food had to be ready to go when the coals were hot. This approach is not so different from the way of cooking that Rita learned by watching her mother cook at home. Rita's mother started cooking on Saturday for the family's Sunday lunchtime meal. Early Sunday morning, when Rita walked into her family's dining room, she saw a flour-covered floor, the table covered with pasta, near ready to be assembled into lasagna.

Most restaurant dishes are a composite of various parts that all come together when the orders arrive from the dining room. Scafata is a good example: this spring contorno, or side dish, features vegetables that need to be washed, shucked, peeled, and trimmed before being sautéed together. To do so, the many ingredients must be prepped ahead of time.

The same principles apply at home. Before you start cooking, look at the dish and think about all the parts. Consider what can be done ahead of time, even a day ahead, to each ingredient to maintain its flavor and integrity until it's ten minutes away from kitchen to table. Artichokes can be poached in large batches and refrigerated. Escarole can be washed and stored in layers between clean dish towels for a maximum of two days. Peas and favas can be shelled (and, in the case of favas, peeled) and stored in airtight containers in the refrigerator for up to two days. **JODY** *&* **RITA**

Stracci con Pesto di Fave

FRESH PASTA SQUARES WITH FAVA PESTO

Hand-cut squares of fresh pasta fold loosely over a fava pesto. The favas can be prepped in stages, and the dish can be put together easily.

SERVES FOUR

piece of Parmigiano Reggiano,
    about 6 ounces/170 grams
salt
extra-virgin olive oil
2 cups/360 grams Fava Pesto
    (page 13)
12 ounces/340 grams Stracci,
    36–40 squares (page 14)

Finely grate the parmigiano (to make about 1¾ cup). Bring a large pot of water to a boil and add 2 tablespoons/20 grams salt. Pour enough oil into a large skillet to coat the bottom and set over medium heat. Add the fava pesto, and stir to warm it through, then turn off the heat.

Cook the pasta squares in two or three batches, giving them a gentle stir to prevent them from sticking together. Cook until slightly al dente, about 2 minutes, lift pasta out of the water with a spider, and add to the pan of pesto. Add a ladle of pasta water (about ½ cup/120 ml) to the pesto and stir to create a loose sauce. Cook the remaining stracci in batches and add to the pesto. Ladle in more water as needed to loosen the sauce, and stir to coat the pasta. Sprinkle with parmigiano before serving.

PESTO DI FAVE

FAVA PESTO

2 large handfuls fresh basil leaves,
    stems removed (about 2 cups)
3 cups/400 grams fava beans
1 tablespoon fresh thyme leaves
    (from about 6 sprigs)
1 cup/100 grams finely grated
    Parmigiano Reggiano
salt
pepper
extra-virgin olive oil

Bring a medium pot of water to a boil and have a bowl of ice water next to the stove. Before you blanch and skin the fava beans, use the water for blanching the basil leaves; salt the water and drop the basil into it. As soon as the leaves turn bright green, about 20 seconds, lift them out of the water with a spider or slotted spoon and drop them into the ice water. Lift them out as soon as they're cool and squeeze the leaves dry on a kitchen towel. Proceed with the fava beans, blanching them in the boiling water for 30 to 60 seconds (as per instructions on page 6) and then dropping them into the ice water.

In a food processor, pulse the basil, favas, and thyme until coarsely chopped. Add the grated parmigiano and pulse a few times, to make a coarse purée. Transfer to a container, season with salt (about 1 teaspoon) and pepper and stir in enough olive oil to lightly bind the pesto (2 to 3 tablespoons/30 to 45 ml). Cover and refrigerate until ready to use, up to 3 days.

STRACCI

FRESH PASTA SQUARES

MAKES ABOUT 40, SERVES FOUR

all-purpose flour or semolina

12 ounces/340 grams Pasta Sfoglia (page 363)

TO ROLL THE STRACCI Have ready a sheet pan lightly dusted with flour or semolina. Have a few clean kitchen towels on hand. It's useful to have a pasta wheel, but a sharp knife will do. Divide the pasta dough into 4 portions. Work with one portion at a time and keep the remaining portions covered with a bowl to prevent them from drying out as you work.

Flatten one portion of dough with the heel of your hand until it's about ½ inch / 1.5 cm thick. Feed it once through the widest setting (#1) of the pasta roller. Fold the dough into thirds and rotate it 90 degrees to pass the narrow side of the rectangle through setting #1 again. Repeat a couple of times until the dough is smooth and even. Adjust the roller to the next setting (#2) and pass the dough through it twice. Feed through each subsequent setting one time until it's thin enough to see the shadow of your hand. Cut the dough into 4 lengths. Lay them flat on the pan, and cover with a kitchen towel. Repeat, keeping the rolled pasta sheets covered while you work.

When all sheets are rolled, cut across at intervals to make rough squares (about 5 inches/13 cm); each pasta sheet will make 10 to 12 pieces. Sprinkle them lightly with flour or semolina and cover with a kitchen towel. If not cooking the pasta right away, cover the pan with a kitchen towel and wrap tightly with plastic wrap. Pasta can be refrigerated for up to 24 hours.

ARTICHOKES

I spent three years cooking in Rome at a little restaurant called Pianeta Terra. It wasn't a typical trattoria; it had one Michelin star and the waiters wore black bow ties and white jackets. When I first knocked on the restaurant's door looking for a job, I said to Roberto, the co-owner and chef, "Sono una brava cuoca"—"I am a good cook." From then on, I had to prove myself day in and day out. I did whatever it took.

The legendary produce market at Campo de' Fiori was practically on the restaurant's doorstep. I walked by the bustling market in the morning on my way to work. The vendors stacked piles of artichokes almost all year, except the hot summer months. There were towers of the long-stemmed, purple ones called violetti di Toscana and bins of the big, round local carciofi Romaneschi. (Romans go crazy for them each spring. They say they are the best artichokes because they have the biggest hearts.)

Often, the sage proprietor who ran the stall, the fruttivendolo, had an assistant who sat on an overturned bucket peeling and trimming artichokes, soaking them in lemon water, and then packing them up. They were sold cleaned and ready to cook.

That was my job at Pianeta Terra. I was the kitchen help. It was a real chore. We went through two or three cases of artichokes a day. They pricked and stained my hands. To this day, my stained, cracked kitchen fingers are a source of pride.

JODY

TIP · TRIMMING ARTICHOKES

Working one artichoke at a time, snap off the tough outer leaves, going around until you reach the softer yellow-green leaves inside. Slice off the top third of each artichoke with a serrated knife or a sharp chef's knife (discard the tops and the outer leaves). Trim the stem, keeping about 1 inch/2–3 cm. If the stems are very long, save them for cooking. Peel the outer layer of the trimmed artichoke bottom and the stems, using a paring knife or vegetable peeler. Slice the artichoke heart in half (unless preparing Carciofi alla Romana, see page 21). Using a teaspoon, scrape out any small, inner leaves, and scoop out the fuzzy choke until the artichoke heart is completely clean. As you work, rub the cut surfaces with a lemon half (or place the trimmed artichokes in a bowl of cold water that has been acidulated with the juice of one lemon).

Carciofi Crudi

SHAVED RAW ARTICHOKES, AVOCADO,
AND BASIL

*We ate a similar salad to this one
at Cipriani in Venice. We then
created our own version. Herbs
and thinly sliced lettuce hearts
are tossed with the artichokes,
and then we add a spoonful
or two of salmoriglio. Choose
very fresh artichokes—the leaves
should be tightly closed and snap
when you pull them off.*

SERVES FOUR

6 baby or 2 full-size artichokes
3 tablespoons/45 ml Salmoriglio
   (page 343)
extra-virgin olive oil
salt
6 fresh basil or mint leaves
1 small, crunchy lettuce heart,
   such as romaine (or 3 leaves)
1 ripe avocado
half a lemon
piece of Parmigiano Reggiano,
   about 2 ounces/55 grams

Trim the artichokes (see page 16 for trimming instructions—but for this recipe be sure to trim the leaves off where they become very tender, because you will be eating the artichokes raw). Once the artichoke hearts are trimmed, slice them very thin. Pat the slices dry on a kitchen towel and then place in a bowl. Toss artichokes with the salmoriglio and a little olive oil (about 2 teaspoons/10 ml) and salt to taste.

Stack the basil or mint leaves on top of each other in an orderly way. Roll them up and draw your knife across them to make fine shreds. Slice the lettuce into wide ribbons; toss the herbs and lettuce with the artichokes. Slice the avocado and add to the bowl; squeeze in a little bit of lemon juice and toss the salad gently; the avocado will become creamy and coat the artichokes. Shave the parmigiano with a vegetable peeler or crumble it with a fork into the salad. Spread the salad in a single layer on a plate and drizzle with olive oil.

Carciofi alla Griglia

GRILLED ARTICHOKES WITH AIOLI

Poaching artichokes ahead of time makes it easy to quickly brown them on a grill or in a hot pan.

SERVES FOUR

12 small (not baby) or 8 full-size
   artichokes
3 quarts/3 liters Court Bouillon
   (page 349)
2 red onions, sliced into thick rings
½ cup/120 ml Salmoriglio
   (page 343)
1 lemon, cut into 4 slices, ends
   discarded
1 cup/240 grams Aioli (page 345)
salt

Trim the artichokes (see page 16 for trimming instructions). If using full-size artichokes, cut them into quarters.

TO POACH THE ARTICHOKES Bring the Court Bouillon to a boil in a medium pot, and gently drop the trimmed artichoke halves into the pot. Stir once to submerge the artichokes and reduce the heat so the bouillon is simmering very gently. Cook the artichokes until they're barely tender, about 20 minutes; the tip of a sharp knife should go into the heart with little resistance. Let the artichokes cool in the poaching liquid. At this point, they can be refrigerated (in their liquid), for 3 days.

TO GRILL Preheat a grill or a grill pan to medium-high. Drain the artichokes and spread onto a clean kitchen towel to dry; discard the court bouillon or save for another use. Season the artichokes and onion slices with salt and brush them with salmoriglio. Grill until browned on both sides, about 3 minutes per side. Grill the lemon slices until lightly charred on both sides, about 4 minutes.

Drizzle salmoriglio over the artichokes, grilled onions, and lemon slices, and serve with aioli for dipping.

Carciofi Fritti

FRIED ARTICHOKES

This is Rita's way of frying artichokes. The artichokes are sliced into thin wedges and dusted with flour. They come out light and crisp.

SERVES FOUR

4 artichokes
all-purpose flour for frying
   (about 1½ cups/180 grams)
salt
extra-virgin olive oil for frying,
   about 3 cups/720 ml
safflower oil for frying, about
   3 cups/720 ml
1 lemon, cut in wedges

Trim the artichokes (see page 16 for trimming instructions). Slice the artichoke halves lengthwise into very thin wedges (about ¼ inch/6 mm). Sift the flour with a good pinch of salt onto a plate. Toss a large handful of artichokes with the flour, making sure they're completely coated; transfer to a sieve to shake off any excess.

Pour equal amounts of olive and safflower oil into a deep, heavy pot until about 3 inches/7–8 cm deep. Heat the oil over high heat for about 8 minutes. Test the oil to see if it's ready; if you drop a breadcrumb into the pot, it should sizzle and float the moment it hits the oil. A candy/deep-fry thermometer clipped on the side of the pot will read 350°F/175°C. While the oil is heating, line a sheet pan with a few layers of paper towel and set it next to the stove.

Gently drop about half the floured artichokes into the hot oil; they should sizzle immediately. Using a spider or tongs, swish the pieces around to keep them from sticking together. Fry until crisp and lightly golden, stirring occasionally, 4 to 5 minutes. Transfer from the oil onto the paper towels and sprinkle lightly with salt.

Repeat with the rest of the artichokes until all are fried, adjusting the heat as needed between batches to maintain the temperature. Serve right away with lemon wedges.

Carciofi alla Romana

BRAISED ARTICHOKES

Slow-cooking artichokes in mint, garlic, anchovies, wine, and olive oil for over an hour is transformational. Serve them at room temperature.

....

SERVES FOUR

6 large artichokes
1 lemon, halved
4 garlic cloves
8 anchovy fillets
handful mint leaves
½ cup/120 ml extra-virgin olive oil
pinch chili flakes
salt
1½ cups/360 ml dry white wine
water if needed

Trim the artichokes (see page 16 for trimming instructions, but instead of slicing the artichokes in half, leave them whole). To remove the choke of the whole, trimmed artichokes, hold the artichoke firmly in the palm of your hand and use both thumbs to push open the leaves, turning and nudging the leaves apart until you can reach the center with a spoon. Scoop out any small, sharp leaves from the heart, using a teaspoon to scrape out the fuzzy choke until the artichoke heart is completely clean. Rub with lemon.

Finely chop the garlic, anchovies, and mint by hand, or pulse in a food processor, adding enough olive oil to help the mixture come together into a coarse pesto (about 3 tablespoons/45 ml). Stir in the chili flakes. Rub this pesto all over the artichokes, inside and out.

Arrange the artichokes upright in a pot large enough to hold them snugly and add any extra stems. Season with ½ teaspoon/ 1.5 grams salt and add a good pour of olive oil (about ⅓ cup/80 ml) and the wine; make sure liquid covers the artichokes by two-thirds; add water if needed.

Bring to a simmer over medium-high, then reduce the heat to low and cook for 10 minutes. Cover the pot and continue cooking until a fork can slide easily into the thickest part of the hearts, 30 to 45 minutes depending on the freshness and size of the artichokes. Uncover the pot occasionally to turn the artichokes in liquid as they cook. (The artichokes can also be cooked this way in the oven—simply place the covered pot in a preheated 375°F/190°C oven.)

Remove from the heat and leave the artichokes to cool in their liquid for at least 20 minutes. The artichokes can be stored in their cooking liquid, refrigerated, up to 3 days.

GREENS

....

There are three things that are often on our table: greens, bread, and olive oil. It's traditional to eat wild greens in springtime all over Italy. Mixtures of spring greens appear in markets; they might include large borage leaves, dandelions, nettles, spinach, wild mustard, and watercress, among others. Dark, wild greens that are rich in minerals are considered tonic for the blood, cleansing and fortifying, especially important in spring. In Rome and throughout the south, bitter greens are widely available most of the year, particularly rugged, cicoria (wild chicory).

There is a section of the Via Carota walk-in that's stacked floor to ceiling with tubs of washed greens. There are buttery, soft heads of lettuce for salads, and for bitterness there are escarole and chicories that we grill, then drizzle with olive oil or Salmoriglio. There are also peppery mustard greens, which we wilt with chard or kale to balance the flavors. Broccoletti (sprouting broccoli) has an intense, mineral-rich verdezza (greenness) and sweet, succulent stalks. Most of the year we have Tuscan kale and Swiss chard on hand. We use all of it: stripping the leaves off the stems, saving the largest stems to go in a soffritto, for the base of soups and legumes, such as our Lenticchie con Cavolo Nero (page 225).

JODY & RITA

Insalata Verde

LEAFY GREENS WITH VIA CAROTA VINAIGRETTE

We are devoted to this salad. We eat it every day. We crave it, in fact, and it is at our dining table nightly. Spring. Summer. Autumn. Winter.

The greens have been purposefully chosen for their different textures and flavors: some sweet and crunchy, others peppery, bitter, or soft. Take good care of your leaves. Wash and dry them gently so they stay crisp. Our objective from the beginning was to create the quintessential green salad. Now, when we look around the dining room, on just about every table, we see a tower of bright green leaves, drizzled with our vinaigrette. We're proud of this bowl of simplicity. It is okay to eat with your hands.

SERVES TWO

1 head of butter lettuce, such as
    Bibb or Boston
a few pieces of frisée (about 6)
2 handfuls little gem lettuce leaves,
    or other crisp lettuce
a small handful peppercress or
    watercress
salt
pepper
¼ cup/60 ml Via Carota
    Vinaigrette (page 340)
3 spears Belgian endive

Pull off any wilted or bruised outer leaves from the butter lettuce. Set aside the floppy, darker green leaves for another use; you will only use the pale inner head. Wash the leaves in two changes of water: First, fill a basin with lukewarm water, and soak the lettuces in it, swishing with your hands. Lift the leaves out and drain in a colander. Second, wash the leaves in cold water, again swishing them with your hands and lifting them out. Rinse the leaves well. Slice the frisée leaves into smaller pieces and separate the little gem leaves and remove any tough stems from the cress; wash them in the same way.

Spin all the leaves dry in a salad spinner, then spread them out on a large, lint-free kitchen towel. In all, you will have about 6 handfuls of mixed leaves. Gently press on them with another towel and roll them up completely.

Place all the leaves in the largest bowl you can find. Season them with a good pinch of salt and a few grindings of pepper. Drizzle in most of the vinaigrette, tossing with your hands to coat the leaves thoroughly.

Lay the leaves on a plate in gradual stages, so they can be piled high without falling. Tuck the endive spears around the sides and drizzle with a little bit more vinaigrette.

Spinaci Saltati

SAUTÉED SPINACH

This is how we make spinach at home in Italy. I like the leaves cooked until they're so soft they feel like silk. If I'm making this for myself, I'll cook it for about 20 minutes. That may be too long for everyone else, so let's say 10 minutes. **RITA**

....

SERVES FOUR

salt

8 handfuls/10 ounces/285 grams
    baby spinach leaves

2 tablespoons/30 ml extra-virgin
    olive oil + more for serving

2 garlic cloves, thinly sliced

chili flakes

Bring a large pot of salted water to a boil. Blanch the spinach, less than 1 minute. Lift it out of the water and transfer to a colander to drain. Press out all the water.

Coat a medium skillet with olive oil and add the garlic and chili flakes. Place over medium-low heat until the garlic is fragrant—do not let it brown. Add the spinach and a pinch of salt and stir well. Reduce the heat to low and cook until all the water is released, and the spinach is very soft, stirring to stop it from sticking to the pan, about 10 minutes.

Scarola e Sarde alla Griglia

GRILLED SARDINES AND ESCAROLE

Sometimes a quick turn over hot coals is the best way to treat your greens. The flames mellow the bracing bitterness of escarole and wilt them quickly. Small fish, like sardines, cook quickly too. If you want to try this recipe indoors, use a heavy grill pan or cast-iron skillet.

SERVES FOUR

2 bunches escarole

salt

extra-virgin olive oil

¼ cup + 2 tablespoons/90 ml Salmoriglio (page 343)

8 fresh sardines, gutted and cleaned

½ cup/100 grams olives such as nocellara or castelvetrano, pitted

Pull off any damaged leaves and cut each head of escarole into 4 to 6 wedges through the core, keeping the leaves attached. Soak the wedges in a bowl of lukewarm water, lift them out, then wash in cold water. Lift out the escarole and shake off the excess water.

Preheat a grill or grill pan over medium-high. Toss the escarole with salt and olive oil. Grill, turning occasionally, until it's wilted and lightly charred in places, 5 to 10 minutes. Cut off the core and toss the leaves in a bowl with salmoriglio (2–3 tablespoons/30–45 ml).

Season the sardines with salt and brush with oil. Scrub the grill or pan clean and lightly oil the grates just before grilling the sardines. Cook until they're charred on both sides and tender when pressed in the center, 4 to 5 minutes total. Spoon salmoriglio over the sardines and escarole on a plate, and scatter olives over them.

Erbazzone

SAVORY SWISS CHARD TART

*At Caffè Arti e Mestieri, where
I cooked in Reggio Emilia,
we made savory tarts filled
with Swiss chard, cavolo nero
(lacinato kale), bietole (beet
greens), or a mixture of wild,
rugged field greens. I learned to
make the classic tart dough with
lard there. In a region known
for prosciutto, what other kind
of fat would you use? Olive oil
makes a golden brown crust too,
and you can use olive oil or lard,
whichever you prefer. Baked on
a sheet pan, this tart is good for
a large gathering or a picnic.
It can be eaten right out of the
oven or at room temperature.*

JODY

MAKES 1 LARGE PIE, SERVES EIGHT

FOR THE CRUST

4 cups/480 grams all-purpose flour

2 teaspoons/6 grams salt

3 tablespoons/45 grams extra-virgin olive oil or lard

1 cup/240 ml water

FOR THE FILLING

1 large bunch Swiss chard

salt

1 pound/454 grams spinach

1 bunch spring onions with greens (or 1 large leek)

¼ cup/60 ml extra-virgin olive oil

2 garlic cloves, finely chopped

1 cup/100 grams finely grated Parmigiano Reggiano

handful fresh flat-leaf parsley leaves, finely chopped

freshly grated nutmeg, about ¼ teaspoon

pepper

FOR THE CRUST In a large bowl, stir the flour
and salt together. Pour in the oil and water
and mix until the dough begins to come
together, adding a splash or two of water if
necessary. (If using lard instead of olive oil,
rub the lard into the flour with your fingertips
before adding the water.) Turn out the dough
onto a work surface and knead lightly until
smooth. Press into an oblong shape, wrap
tightly with plastic, or parchment paper, and
refrigerate for 1 hour.

FOR THE FILLING Strip the Swiss chard leaves from the ribs. Finely chop the stems and tear the leaves into large pieces. Add the chard stems to a large pot of generously salted, boiling water and cook for 2 minutes. Then add the chard leaves and spinach to the pot, pressing to submerge. Cook in two batches if necessary. Cook until greens are soft, about 2 minutes. Drain in a colander and repeat with the remaining greens. When cool enough to handle, press out as much water as possible.

Finely chop the spring onions, including the greens. (If using leeks, discard tough outer layer and wash the leeks in two changes of water after chopping.) Heat the oil in a large skillet over medium heat and add the oil, onions, and garlic and a pinch of salt. Cook until the onions are very soft, 8 to 10 minutes; don't let them brown. Raise the heat to medium-high, add the chard and spinach, and cook, stirring, until the water has evaporated, about 5 minutes. Transfer to a large bowl and cool to room temperature. Stir in the parmigiano, parsley, and nutmeg. Season with salt and pepper.

Preheat the oven to 400°F/200°C. Line a sheet pan (18 x 13 inches/45 x 33 cm) with parchment paper. Divide the dough in two, and on a lightly floured surface, roll one half into a thin sheet large enough to cover the pan, with a little bit of overhang (keep the second dough covered while you work).

Spread the greens in an even layer onto the dough, leaving the edges bare. Roll out the second piece of dough and lay it on top, pressing into the sides of the pan. Firmly crimp the edges together and prick the top of the pie all over with the tines of a fork, making sure to go all the way to the bottom. Lightly brush the surface with olive oil, and bake until the pie is golden, 25 to 30 minutes. Let cool on a wire rack for at least 15 minutes, cut into large squares, and serve.

ASPARAGUS

....

Asparagus in the spring—who could want for
more? Choose firm spears with good tips. Keep
them upright in a container with a little bit of
water and they will stay fresh for a few days.

Asparagi alla Fiorentina

GREEN ASPARAGUS AND POACHED EGGS

There is nothing extra in this understated dish, so each ingredient needs to stand on its own. Cooking the asparagus and eggs correctly takes some concentration at the stove, and it happens quickly. Give them your complete focus, and don't walk away while they're cooking.

....

SERVES TWO

salt
8 thick spears asparagus, trimmed,
    and peeled up to the tips
pepper
extra-virgin olive oil
2 large eggs
piece of Parmigiano Reggiano,
    about 2 ounces/55 grams

Fill a medium sauté pan halfway with water, stir in 1 teaspoon/3 grams salt, and bring to a boil. Lay the asparagus in the water in a single layer and reduce heat to medium-low so the water is at a simmer. Cook until asparagus is vivid green—a fork should meet only slight resistance, about 3 minutes.

While the asparagus is cooking, fill a medium saucepan with water and heat over medium-low so the water is barely simmering.

When the asparagus is done, lift it out of the water, divide between two plates, season with salt and pepper, and drizzle with olive oil. Keep warm while you poach the eggs.

Stir the water in a circular motion to create a whirlpool in the center. Crack 1 egg into a small cup and, with the cup just above the pot, tip out the egg into the swirling water. Repeat with the second egg, making sure the whites do not touch. Rotate the eggs with a spoon and cook until the white is a thin veil over the yolk, 1 minute and 20 seconds.

Lift the eggs out with a slotted spoon and place on a kitchen towel to blot the water; trim off any straggly bits. Add eggs to the plates, and season eggs and asparagus with salt and pepper. Serve drizzled with olive oil and sprinkled with grated parmigiano.

Carpaccio di Asparagi Bianchi

SHAVED RAW WHITE ASPARAGUS
WITH AGED BALSAMIC

*White asparagus appears for
a short time in May. It has a
delicate flavor, and we serve
it raw with our best balsamic
vinegar. The stalks should be
firm with ends that are not
dry or shriveled. Shaved with a
vegetable peeler, the asparagus
will fall onto the cutting board
in fine ribbons.*

....

SERVES FOUR

8 thick spears white asparagus
extra-virgin olive oil
salt
pepper
piece of Parmigiano Reggiano,
    about 4 ounces/115 grams
1–2 tablespoons/15–30 ml Via
    Carota Vinaigrette (page 340)
aged balsamic vinegar tradizionale

Snap off the bottoms of the asparagus and
peel the exterior with a vegetable peeler. One
by one, hold the asparagus spears firmly
and shave them into strips. When you have
shaved an asparagus spear down to a small
piece, use a knife to finish slicing it.

Lay about half of the asparagus on a plate,
drizzle with olive oil, and sprinkle with salt
and pepper. Repeat with the remaining
asparagus, oil, salt, and pepper. Use a peeler
to shave long, thin shards of parmigiano over
the asparagus, covering them completely.
Spoon a little bit of vinaigrette over the
salad and sprinkle judiciously with balsamic
vinegar.

PLATING

I remember one morning when I stopped in to visit Rita during brunch at I Sodi and she was sending out plates of asparagi alla fiorentina to the dining room. I watched one of the cooks put asparagus on each plate. Rita stood at the corner stove, and with great care, poached each egg, one by one, and placed them on top of the asparagus.

JODY

EGGS

IL POLLAIO

Growing up, my family had a pollaio, a henhouse. We kept around twenty chicken coops in there—and ducks and turkeys, too. It was my job to collect the eggs from the pollaio every day. I used to feel around in the warm straw with my hand where each hen had been sitting and came back to the house with the eggs in my wicker basket. I felt proud. My mother stored them in a special egg shelf on the wall. The eggs came in all sizes and the shells in different colors. When we ate them, the yolks were so yellow, it was almost like a sunrise. Every now and then we had double yolks, and sometimes a little red spot where an egg had been fertilized. I knew we ate the birds too. As I got older, I was spared killing them— that work fell to my father, Pietro. My mother did the plucking and cleaning. These were not pleasant tasks, but they had to be done. You learn about the cycle of life when you're raised on a farm. It begins with the egg.

RITA

Frittata d'Ortica

FRITTATA WITH NETTLES AND RICOTTA

Should we make a thin frittata or a thick one? We can't decide. Some days Jody likes a thin one you can cook on the stovetop without even flipping. Rita likes a thicker one she cooks slowly over low heat on the stovetop before finishing in a hot oven. We both like our frittata creamy, with ricotta inside and parmigiano on top. The recipe that follows is Rita's thicker frittata. Adding iron-rich nettles—also Rita's choice—feels right for a spring frittata; they're some of the first greens of the season.

SERVES TWO

6 large eggs
½ teaspoon/1.5 grams salt
¼ cup/25 grams grated Parmigiano Reggiano + more for serving
½ cup/50 grams cooked nettles or other dark greens (see below)
extra-virgin olive oil
¼ cup/60 grams ricotta

Preheat the oven to 400°F/200°C. Whisk the eggs until thoroughly blended. Stir in the salt, parmigiano, and cooked nettles. Heat a small (8 inch/20 cm) skillet over low heat and add a generous pour of olive oil, swirling the pan to coat the bottom and sides. Pour in the egg mixture and cook without stirring for 1 minute. Then push the eggs with a spatula, bringing the sides into the center and tipping the pan slightly to let the uncooked egg fill the edges. Spoon dollops of ricotta on top, and let the eggs cook undisturbed until the edges are set, about 2 minutes. Transfer the pan to the oven and cook until the frittata is puffed but the center is still slightly runny, about 8 minutes. Place on a cooling rack and cover with a plate for 5 minutes to set the center. Remove the plate and run a knife around the sides and bottom of the pan.

Now you can either lift your frittata from the skillet directly onto a plate or flip it to see the golden-brown bottom. To flip, hold the plate firmly on top and invert the skillet swiftly so the frittata drops onto it. Serve with a dusting of freshly grated parmigiano.

HOW TO PREPARE NETTLES

Wild nettles are used culinarily for their purifying properties; they're potent in flavor, too, with a deep, savory taste. Approach nettles with caution: wear gloves to protect your hands from the sting. Once cooked, they are completely tame.

....

MAKES ABOUT ½ CUP/
50 GRAMS

1 bunch (about 3 cups) nettles
salt
extra-virgin olive oil
1 large garlic clove, thinly sliced
pinch of chili flakes

Chop nettles into lengths about 4 inches/ 10 cm and discard the thickest stems. Soak in a bowl of lukewarm water twice, lifting them out with a strainer each time before refilling the bowl. Rinse with cool water.

Bring a pot of salted water to a boil and stir in the nettles; cook until the stems are soft, about 3 minutes. Lift out of the water with a spider or strainer. Drain the nettles, pressing out all the water. Coarsely chop them.

Coat a skillet with olive oil and add the garlic and pinch of chili flakes. Heat over medium until the garlic is light brown and fragrant. Add the nettles and toss well. Cook until all the water is released, and the nettles are very soft, about 15 minutes, stirring occasionally and adding a little olive oil if the pan seems dry.

MERENDA

At almost any time of day, I can eat a frittata panino:
wedges of cool frittata eaten between slices of bread
or stuffed into a roll. Drizzle the frittata with olive oil
and sprinkle with flaky sea salt before sandwiching it.
This was my merenda, or school snack, growing up.
My mother would make a frittata in the morning,
then she would turn it into a sandwich. She'd stuff
the fritatta between two pieces of bread while it was
still warm, then wrap it in brown paper. By the time
I ate the sandwich at school, it was a little soggy.
Good soggy. I wish people could be lucky like I was
at that time.

RITA

Tortino di Carciofi

EGG NEST WITH ARTICHOKES

A tortino is a nest-shaped frittata. By swirling the pan in a steady motion over the heat, the eggs are gathered into loose ribbons that fold on top of each other, wrapping around the artichokes in the center. It takes two hands and complete concentration. The best pan for this is a 2 quart/2 liter saucepan with high sides. Practice, practice, practice.

....

MAKES I TORTINO,
SERVES ONE TO TWO

I full-size artichoke

3 large eggs

salt

2 tablespoons/15 grams finely
    grated Parmigiano Reggiano
    + more for serving

extra-virgin olive oil

flaky sea salt for sprinkling

Read these directions to the end before you begin. You will work in one continuous motion, pouring the eggs into the hot oil in three additions. Keep the pan tilted on one corner to avoid browning the bottom.

For I tortino: Trim the artichoke (see page 16 for trimming instructions). Slice the artichoke halves into wedges as thin as you can make them (about ⅛ inch/3 mm). Pat the slices dry with a kitchen towel. Whisk the eggs with a pinch of salt and the parmigiano.

Generously coat a medium saucepan with oil (at least 2 tablespoons), and place over high heat until shimmering. Add a small handful of artichoke slices (you won't use the entire artichoke for this recipe) and cook until golden, about 2 minutes. Season with salt.

Tilt the saucepan at an angle, so the artichokes are in one corner. With the pot still tilted (only one edge touching the burner), pour about a third of the egg mixture into the hottest corner, behind the artichokes. Swirl the pot slowly until the eggs coat the bottom and gather the artichokes as they cook. Loosen the eggs and shake them to one corner of the pot. Keep the pot tilted with only one edge on the burner and pour the remaining eggs onto the cooked eggs in two additions, rolling the pot slowly and continuously as you pour, until all of the eggs are combined.

Remove from the heat right away, and cover the pot for a minute if the eggs are very runny. Sprinkle the finished tortino with flaky sea salt, drizzle with olive oil, and shower with parmigiano.

SOSTANZA

Oh, to be lucky enough to go out for dinner in Florence, where we can be spectators instead of chefs. One of our favorite sources of inspiration is Trattoria Sostanza, known among the locals as Il Troia. We soak up the atmosphere of this timeless place—along with a lot of wine. We get to taste so many things when we go with Rita's family, ten or more people. We watch the owner and host slice prosciutto and finocchiona, the local salami, on the narrow bar near the front door. We watch the cooks in their tiny kitchen, making the tortino di carciofi on their smoking-hot 100-year-old coal stove. At home, we practice making the same dish over and over until we get it right.

JODY

Stracciatella

CHICKEN SOUP WITH EGG CLOUDS

Stracciatella helps chase off an early-spring chill, and it will placate picky children and hungover adults. Finely grated parmigiano is key to creating the ideal texture for the stracci— "rags"—that swirl in the soup. Grate your cheese into a powder on the smallest holes of a grater to create little shreds of egg that are as light as clouds.

SERVES FOUR

1 small yellow onion

2 medium carrots

2 celery stalks

2 large chicken thighs or 1 split
   chicken breast (bone-in)

6 cups/1.5 liters chicken stock,
   preferably homemade

salt

3 large eggs, lightly beaten

¼ cup/25 grams finely grated
   Parmigiano Reggiano + more
   for serving

8 handfuls/10 ounces/285 grams
   baby spinach leaves

extra-virgin olive oil

pepper

Dice the onion, carrots, and celery into medium pieces (about ¾ inch/2 cm) and place in a medium pot. Add the chicken and stock. Bring to a boil and immediately reduce the heat to medium-low, so the stock is barely simmering. Use a large spoon to skim any foam from the surface. Simmer until the chicken is just cooked through, about 25 minutes. Add salt as needed. Remove the chicken from the pot and set it aside on a plate until cool enough to handle. Take the meat off the bones and pull it into pieces; return to the pot.

Whisk the eggs with the ¼ cup/25 grams parmigiano and ½ teaspoon/1.5 grams salt in a medium bowl until thoroughly blended. With the chicken stock gently simmering, use one hand to pour the egg mixture into the stock in a steady stream while the other hand stirs with a wooden spoon: 1, 2, 3 times, until the eggs set into small shreds. Stir the spinach into the soup and turn off the heat. Taste for salt.

Ladle into bowls and drizzle with olive oil. Grind pepper into each bowl and sprinkle with parmigiano. Pass more cheese at the table.

LAMB

Young lamb is abundant in Italy during the spring. The stalls at the vibrant outdoor markets sell lamb shanks, lamb heads, and whole lambs. Every table is graced with a lamb dish on Easter Sunday in a country rooted in religious traditions dating back to ancient Roman civilization. A whole roasted lamb, or abbacchio, is the most traditional. Motor scooters crisscross the cities and small countryside communities as locals, with lambs strapped to their backs, head home.

JODY

Agnello in Gremolata

BRAISED LAMB SHOULDER WITH LEMON ZEST

SERVES SIX

1 boneless lamb shoulder
     (about 3 pounds/1.4 kg)

salt

pepper

extra-virgin olive oil

2 garlic cloves, lightly crushed

1 sprig fresh rosemary

about ¼ cup/60 ml dry white wine

2 tablespoons/30 grams capers,
     optional, rinsed

6 green olives, such as
     castelvetrano, optional, rinsed

2 cups/480 ml water

Gremolata for serving (see below)

Preheat the oven to 350°F/175°C. Season the lamb generously with salt and pepper. In a large Dutch oven set over medium-high heat, brown the lamb on all sides in olive oil. Add the crushed garlic cloves and rosemary and cook until the garlic is golden. Add the white wine and let it evaporate. If using, add the capers and olives. Pour in the water, and bring to a boil.

Cover the pot, transfer to the oven, and roast until the juices have mostly reduced, about 2½ to 3 hours. Add a splash of water to the pot if it seems dry.

Check for doneness: the meat should pull apart with two forks with little effort. If it doesn't, cover and return to the oven for as long as needed. Spoon gremolata and any pan juices over thick slices of lamb.

GREMOLATA

A sprinkle of lemon zest with chopped parsley and garlic is traditional for the lamb. We think it's nice to add juice from the lemon and stir in olive oil, to make a condiment to spoon over the meat.

. . . .

MAKES ABOUT ½ CUP/
120 GRAMS

large handful fresh flat-leaf parsley

1 lemon

2 garlic cloves

extra-virgin olive oil

salt

pepper

Wash and dry the parsley, discarding the thickest stems. Chop the parsley, including remaining stems. Transfer to a medium bowl. Zest the lemon over the bowl and then squeeze in the juice. Finely grate the garlic into the bowl and pour in enough olive oil to make the gremolata loose. Season with salt and pepper as needed.

Cosciotto di Agnello
al Forno

ROAST LEG OF LAMB WITH NEW POTATOES

This roast is fitting for a spring celebration. You will need kitchen twine for tying the lamb.

....

SERVES SIX

1 boneless, butterflied leg of lamb,
    about 3.5 pounds/1.5 kg

salt

pepper

6 large garlic cloves

4 rosemary sprigs

extra virgin olive oil

1.5 pounds/700 grams new
    potatoes, or other thin-skinned
    boiling potatoes

half a lemon

At least 1 hour, and up to 24 hours before you wish to cook the lamb, unfold it and season all over with salt and pepper. Peel the garlic cloves and crush them slightly by pressing down firmly with the flat side of a knife. Lay the garlic and the rosemary sprigs onto the cut side of the lamb, pressing the garlic into any crevices, and roll up the leg. Rub the exterior lightly with olive oil and refrigerate if more than 2 hours before roasting. About 1 hour before roasting, set the lamb on a lightly oiled sheet pan and bring to room temperature. With the rounded side facing up (and the fat on top), tie kitchen twine around the lamb 3 or 4 times to hold it snugly.

Preheat the oven to 450°F/230°C with a rack in the center. Scrub the potatoes clean, and cut them in half, or quarter if large. Place potatoes in a medium saucepan with cold water to cover, and season generously with salt. Boil the potatoes until barely tender when pierced, about 10 minutes. Drain in a colander, and return to the hot pot; shake the pot and set it on the stove with the burner off to dry the potatoes. Roast the lamb until you hear it sizzling and smell the rosemary, 15 to 20 minutes. Reduce the oven temperature to 350°F/170°C and take the pan out of the oven. Spread the potatoes around the lamb, and stir to coat with fat. Continue roasting until the internal temperature of the lamb reaches 125°F/52°C for medium rare, about 30 minutes more.

Transfer the lamb and potatoes to a platter; cover them lightly with foil and rest for 10 to 15 minutes before slicing. Meanwhile, pour a good splash of water into the roasting pan and squeeze in the juice of the half lemon. Set the pan over a medium-high burner and bring to a simmer, stirring up the browned bits from the pan. Add salt and pepper as needed, and pour this sauce over the sliced lamb and potatoes.

RAMPS AND GARLIC SCAPES

We work with wild, pungent ramps early in spring when foragers deliver them to our door. They're sizzled on the grill with pancetta or wilted into Scafata (page 9) or a frittata. Later in the season, garlic scapes, the twisted shoots of hard-neck garlic, arrive in the markets. We like their mild garlic flavor and unusual look, and we cook them until tender in a pot of beans.

Ramps

RAMPS WITH PANCETTA AND POLENTA

We bring out the sweetness of ramps by grilling them with salty pancetta. We unceremoniously pile the ramps onto the grill with the pancetta on top. While some ramps are getting charred, others are getting steamed, and the fat is melting over everything.

....

SERVES FOUR

6 cups/1.5 liters water
salt
1⅔ cups/225 grams polenta
  (not quick-cooking) or
  medium-coarse cornmeal
16 ramps
extra-virgin olive oil
6 thin slices pancetta (2 ounces/
  55 grams)
3 tablespoons/45 ml Via Carota
  Vinaigrette (page 340)

FOR THE POLENTA Bring a saucepan of salted water to a boil. Put the polenta in a cup with a spout: with whisk in one hand and the cup in the other, pour the polenta into the boiling water in a slow stream, whisking constantly. Reduce the heat to low and continue whisking until the polenta has been incorporated (you should no longer see a layer of water above the polenta), about 5 minutes. Adjust the heat as needed so the polenta is bubbling occasionally. Switch to a wooden spoon to stir every few minutes. Polenta is ready when it's thick enough to hold a slight trail when stirred, about 40 minutes; the grains should be soft on your tongue. Add salt as needed.

Set a straight-sided dish, about 9 x 7 inches/ 23 x 18 cm, next to the stove. Pour the polenta into the dish to cool it until firm, about 1 hour. Now you can cut it for grilling or cover the dish and refrigerate it for up to 2 days.

Soak the ramps twice in a bowl of warm water, lifting them out after each soak and refilling the bowl. Follow with a rinse in cold water and check the ends for any remaining soil. Drain, and toss lightly with salt and olive oil.

Preheat a grill or a grill pan to medium-high, scrub clean, and brush with oil. Cut the polenta into 3 inch/7.5cm squares and brush the tops with oil. Place each square top side down on the grill. Cook until the bottom can be lifted without tearing, about 5 minutes; don't try to turn the polenta before it's ready. Brush the polenta with oil and flip it with a spatula; grill on the second side until heated through, 5 minutes. Transfer to a plate and keep warm.

Lay the ramps in a pile on the grill or grill pan. Drape the pancetta slices on top of the ramps and grill until the pancetta begins to sizzle and melt onto the ramps, about 4 minutes. Flip the pile so the pancetta is on the bottom and cook until it's crisp—don't worry about the ramps being evenly browned. Transfer to a bowl and toss with 2 tablespoons/30 ml vinaigrette.

Pile the ramps on top of the polenta and spoon more dressing over them. Arrange the pancetta on top.

Scapi di Aglio con Fagioli

GARLIC SCAPES WITH LIMA BEANS

We admire the look of green garlic scapes with the budding garlic at the end. We cut them long to keep their curving shapes intact.

....

SERVES FOUR

2 cups/about 340 grams dried large lima beans or gigante beans
extra-virgin olive oil
salt
8 garlic scapes

Spread the beans out on a plate to look for any clumps of soil or pebbles, then rinse the beans well. Place them in a container with enough space for them to triple in size and cover them with about 3 inches/7.5 cm cold water. Soak overnight in the refrigerator.

The next day, discard any floating beans or skins and drain the beans. Place them in a medium pot (you'll need enough space for them to double in size), cover with cold water by about 2 inches/5 cm, and bring to a boil. Skim off any foam that rises to the top, then add a good pour of olive oil (about 3 tablespoons/60 ml) and reduce the heat to low so the beans are simmering gently. Cover the pot and cook until tender, about 30 to 45 minutes, or longer depending on the freshness of the beans. Stir in about 2 teaspoons/6 grams of salt and continue cooking for 10 to 15 more minutes to allow the beans to absorb the salt.

Drain the beans over a bowl and reserve the liquid (if not using them right away, cool the beans in their liquid). Cooked beans can be refrigerated in their liquid up to 5 days, or frozen for 1 month.

Trim the garlic scapes at the point where they become soft enough to bend (about 2 inches/5 cm). Discard the tough bottoms and any dried tips. Slice the scapes in three pieces. Coat a medium saucepan with olive oil and heat over medium; cook the garlic scapes in the oil, about 3 minutes. Stir in the drained beans and just enough liquid to cover them (about 2 cups/480 ml), taste for salt, and reduce the heat to medium-low. Cook until the scapes are tender, 20 to 25 minutes. Serve the beans and scapes in their cooking liquid.

PEAS

The sweetest peas are small and tender. Buy peas
in their pods at the peak of the season. Ideally, the
pods should be taut and unblemished. Naturally,
the pods keep the peas inside fresh and moist,
so shell them the same day you want to cook
them. When buying peas in their pods, estimate
that 1 pound/454 grams will yield about 1 cup/
130 grams shelled peas. We often add prosciutto
crudo or prosciutto cotto when we prepare a dish
of peas; there is harmony when the sweet and salty
come together.

Panini con Piselli

LITTLE SANDWICHES OF PEAS, MASCARPONE,
AND PROSCIUTTO COTTO

*Choose a good ham (prosciutto
cotto). We use a thinly sliced
baked ham, not a cured or
smoked one.*

MAKES 8 SMALL SANDWICHES,
SERVES FOUR

1 cup/130 grams shelled peas
   (from 1 pound/454 grams
   peas in their pods)
salt
pepper
about 2 teaspoons extra-virgin
   olive oil
8 mini sandwich rolls, such as
   brioche
4 ounces/115 grams mascarpone
½ pound/225 grams thinly sliced
   prosciutto cotto, or other ham,
   optional

Bring a small pot of salted water to a
boil and add the peas; cook until bright
and just tender, 30 seconds to 2 minutes,
depending on freshness and size of the peas.
Drain the peas, toss them in a bowl with salt,
pepper, and olive oil, and spread them out on
a plate to cool for five minutes.

Split the rolls in half and spread mascarpone
on the bottom halves. Spoon peas on top.
Add a few slices of prosciutto cotto or
other ham.

Insalata di Piselli

LEAFY GREENS, SWEET PEAS, AND PROSCIUTTO

This salad is piled high and bright green—spring on a plate.

....

SERVES TWO

1 cup/130 grams shelled peas

salt

pepper

extra-virgin olive oil

6 fresh mint leaves

6 fresh basil leaves

2 heads butter lettuce, such as
    Bibb or Boston

2 handfuls little gem lettuce leaves,
    or other crisp lettuce

handful pea shoots

½ cup/120 ml Robiola Vinaigrette
    (page 341)

6 thin slices prosciutto di Parma

Bring a small pot of salted water to a boil and add the peas; cook until bright, from 30 seconds to 2 minutes, depending on freshness and the size of the peas. Drain the peas, toss them in a bowl with salt, pepper, and a little olive oil (about 1 teaspoon), and spread them out on a plate to cool for five minutes. Tear the mint and basil leaves into small pieces and stir into the peas.

Pull off any wilted or bruised outer leaves from the butter lettuce. Set aside the floppy, darker green leaves for another use; you will only use the pale inner head. Wash the leaves in two changes of water: First, fill a basin with lukewarm water and soak both lettuces in it, swishing with your hands. Lift the leaves out and drain in a colander. Second, wash the leaves in cold water, again swishing them with your hands and lifting them out. Rinse the leaves well. Spin all the leaves dry in a salad spinner, then lay them out on a large, lint-free kitchen towel. In all, you will have 5 to 6 handfuls of mixed leaves. Gently press on them with another towel and roll them up completely.

Place the leaves and pea shoots in the largest bowl you can find. Season them with a large pinch of salt and a few grindings of pepper. Add the dressing gradually while tossing with your hands to coat the leaves thoroughly. Layer the salad on a plate in stages, tucking the prosciutto in between the leaves as you go. Spoon the peas on top.

Risi e Bisi

RICE AND PEAS

A Venetian classic that relies only on fresh, sweet peas and the best short-grain, Italian rice. We choose vialone nano rice. Prosciutto is optional. Risi e bisi falls somewhere between a soup and a risotto.

....

SERVES FOUR

6–7 cups/1.5–1.7 liters Pea Pod Stock (page 61), Vegetable Broth (page 348), or water

extra-virgin olive oil

½ cup finely diced prosciutto ends (about 2 ounces/55 grams), optional

½ medium yellow onion, finely chopped

1 cup/200 grams risotto rice, such as vialone nano

½ cup/120 ml dry white wine

salt

1¼ cups/180 grams shelled peas (from 1¼ pounds/570 grams pea pods)

2 tablespoons/28 grams unsalted butter

⅓ cup/35 grams finely grated Parmigiano Reggiano + more for serving

Bring the stock or water to a simmer in a medium pot. Coat the bottom of a wide saucepan with oil (about 2 tablespoons/30 ml) and place over medium heat. Add the prosciutto (if using) and onions and cook until softened but not browned, 6 or 7 minutes. Add the rice and stir with a wooden spoon until the grains are coated with oil and glossy, about 2 minutes. Pour in the wine and simmer until it's absorbed by the rice, stirring to prevent it from sticking to the pan.

Add 1 teaspoon/3 grams salt to the stock or water. Pour a ladle of stock (about ½ cup/120 ml) into the rice and stir until it's completely absorbed. Add hot stock or water one ladleful at a time, only adding more when the rice is ready to absorb more (you will know it's ready when the bubbling increases and the spoon leaves a slow trail in the rice). Stir after each addition of stock and cook until the rice is almost tender, about 18 minutes (you will still have some stock left in the pot).

Stir in the peas with a pinch of salt and gradually add more stock (about 1 cup/240 ml). Cook until the peas are bright and just tender, 1 to 2 minutes. Add more stock to loosen the rice as needed. Stir in the butter to melt, add the parmigiano, and cover the pot. Turn off the heat and let the risi e bisi sit for 2 minutes to settle. Serve with a dusting of parmigiano.

PEA POD STOCK (VARIATION)

After shelling peas for Risi e Bisi (page 60),
Insalata di Piselli (page 59), or anything else
that uses them, save the pods. Wash them in
cool water and rinse well.

Prepare a pot of Vegetable Broth (page 348),
making sure you have some extra space in
the pot. Add 2 extra cups/480 ml of water.
After 1 hour add the pods to the simmering
vegetable broth and press to submerge them.
Cook for 30 minutes. Strain through a sieve
and discard the solids; store the stock up to
2 days in the refrigerator.

CARROTS AND BEETS

Both carrots and beets have a growing season that begins in late spring and continues through the warmer months here in the East. They're especially sweet and tender in the spring. Once roasted they take well to lemony salmoriglio, fresh herb leaves, sheep's and goat's milk cheeses, and creamy yogurt, all of which highlight their sweetness.

Carote

ROASTED CARROTS, SPICED YOGURT,
AND PISTACHIOS

This roasted carrot dish has been a favorite since we opened, and we don't dare take it off the menu. We add a crunch of pistachios and cumin, not traditionally Italian—this is Jody's tweak.

....

SERVES FOUR

2 cups/500 ml water

1 tablespoon/12 grams sugar

1 pound/454 grams multicolored
   carrots (about 8), peeled

salt

extra-virgin olive oil

¾ teaspoon/2 grams cumin seeds,
   toasted and coarsely ground

⅓ cup/80 ml Salmoriglio
   (page 343)

¼ cup/35 grams toasted
   pistachios, chopped

½ cup/120 grams full-fat Greek
   yogurt

large handful mixed fresh herbs,
   such as basil, mint, cilantro,
   parsley, and chives

Preheat the oven to 450°F/230C°. Stir water and sugar in a large baking dish to dissolve the sugar and add the carrots, coating them. Tightly cover the dish with foil and place it in the oven to steam the carrots until they're tender when pierced with a fork, about 30 minutes. Drain off any water remaining in the dish, toss the carrots with salt, and lightly coat with olive oil. Spread the carrots out in the dish and return to the oven, uncovered, to roast until browned, about 20 minutes. While the carrots are hot, toss them with about half the cumin, half the salmoriglio, and the pistachios. Season the yogurt with salt and the rest of the cumin and spoon it onto a plate. Arrange the carrots on the yogurt and spoon the remaining salmoriglio over them. Refresh the herb leaves briefly in a bowl of ice water and pat them dry before piling loosely on top.

TIP · TOASTING NUTS AND SPICES

Toasting nuts and spices brings out their aromatic oils. It's a small step that enhances any dish. You can usually toast spices in the same skillet you will use to cook. Toss them in a dry pan over medium heat until they're fragrant, about 2 minutes. Give the pan a shake to toss the spices and then remove from the heat. Toasting for too long makes them bitter.

   Nuts toast most evenly on a sheet pan in the oven; it takes less than 10 minutes in a moderate oven (350°F/180°C). Watch them carefully, and use your nose to tell you when they're done—they should smell nutty and toasted but not acrid. Just like spices, once they become very dark they become bitter. Cool the nuts on a plate, not in the pan.

THE DOOR KNOCKER

On the back of the worn wooden kitchen door at the
house on Via del Carota was a very old bronze door
knocker. I like to imagine the many hands that had
touched it over the years. Of the countless memories
I hold on to from that time, it is this door knocker
that brings me back. I took a photograph of it as I
left the house for the last time in the spring of 2012.
Its strength and integrity continue to inspire our
vision and the soul of Via Carota.

JODY

Barbabietole alla Scapece

BEETS MARINATED IN VINEGAR AND MINT

This is a remarkably hands-off approach to preparing beets; aside from making sure they're very clean before you cook them, there is no prep needed. The beets' skins are nutritious. Healthy greens are a sign of freshness—use those too.

....

SERVES FOUR

1 pound/454 grams small or
    medium beets
extra-virgin olive oil
salt
pepper
4 beet leaves, if fresh
¼ cup/60 ml aged sherry vinegar
1 small red onion, halved and thinly
    sliced
2 garlic cloves, thinly sliced
handful fresh mint leaves, torn
    + more for serving

Preheat the oven to 400°F/200°C. Trim the beets and scrub them well, removing any debris or rough spots. Rinse well. Reserve any nice leaves and wash in cold water. Spin the leaves dry and then finely slice them. Cut the beets into quarters, or halves if small. Transfer to a sheet pan, toss with enough olive oil to coat (about 2 tablespoons), and sprinkle generously with salt and pepper. Roast until the beets are tender when pierced with a fork, 45 minutes to 55 minutes.

Combine the vinegar, onions, and garlic in a medium bowl. Stir in the hot beets, sliced leaves (if using), and the mint leaves; toss well. Season with salt and pepper as needed. Leave to marinate in the refrigerator for at least 2 hours, preferably overnight, and stir a few times while they're marinating. Serve at room temperature with fresh mint leaves on top.

RHUBARB AND STRAWBERRIES

Together, rhubarb and strawberries bridge the spring and early summer. One is tart, the other sweet—they're a natural pairing.

The rosiest field-grown rhubarb usually appears in April. Before then, we make sure to mix a few red stalks with the paler ones in every batch we cook. We prefer slim, firm stalks; if we have very large ones, we peel off the stringy fibers with a vegetable peeler. We cook rhubarb with as little sugar as needed to sweeten it without losing its sour.

Color is one of the best indicators of a strawberry's sweetness—the deeper red they are, the better. There should be no sign of a hard, white core around the leaves. We look for berries that are plump and have a little bit of shine. A great variety grown here in New York is called the Tristar. They're small and round, sweet, and very red. Our local farmers plant a September crop in addition to the late-spring one, so we get a second chance to enjoy them.

Bevanda di Fragole e Rabarbaro

STRAWBERRY-RHUBARB SPRITZ

MAKES 2

10 small, ripe strawberries (about
    6 ounces/170 grams)
2 ounces/60 ml Rhubarb Syrup
    (recipe below)
ice
4 ounces/120 ml white vermouth
    (not dry), such as Contratto
    Bianco or Cocchi Americano
    Bianco
2 teaspoons/10 ml fresh lemon
    juice (from half a lemon)
sparkling water

Rinse the strawberries and set two aside for garnish. Hull the rest, and slice into quarters. In a cocktail shaker (or a large jar with a tight-fitting lid), muddle the strawberries and the rhubarb syrup. Fill the shaker with ice and pour in the vermouth and lemon juice. Put on the lid and shake vigorously for about 4 seconds. Strain or pour into two ice-filled rocks glasses and top up each drink with sparkling water. Drop a strawberry into each glass and serve.

MAKES ABOUT 12 OUNCES/
360 ML

½ pound/225 grams red rhubarb
    (about 4 stalks)
1 cup/200 grams sugar
salt
1 cup/240 ml sparkling water

FOR THE RHUBARB SYRUP

Rinse the rhubarb and cut into short lengths (about 1 inch/2.5 cm). Combine the rhubarb with the sugar, a small pinch of salt, and the water in a small pot. Cook over medium-low heat, stirring until the sugar dissolves (about 5 minutes), then turn off the heat. Let the syrup cool to room temperature, about 30 minutes. Strain through a fine-mesh sieve, pressing to extract all the syrup from the rhubarb. Discard the rhubarb (or save for another use). Rhubarb syrup can be refrigerated for up to 1 week.

Conserva di Rabarbaro

RHUBARB COMPOTE

Spoon this seasonal compote on top of Torta di Ricotta (page 76) or stir into a bowl of creamy yogurt in the morning.

....

MAKES 2 CUPS/500 ML

1 pound/454 grams rhubarb
⅓ cup/65 grams sugar
¼ cup/60 ml water

Rinse the rhubarb, trim the ends, and cut the stalks into 1 inch/2.5 cm pieces (you will have about 4 cups). Place rhubarb and sugar in a medium saucepan, pour in the water, and place over medium heat. Stir occasionally as the rhubarb comes to a simmer and releases its liquid. The rhubarb will soften quickly; cook until the liquid is foamy and the pieces are soft, about 5 minutes. Remove from the heat and pour into a nonreactive bowl to cool. Rhubarb compote can be refrigerated for up to 1 week.

RICOTTA

In Sicily and regions south of Rome, ricotta is usually made from sheep's milk, while most American ricotta is made from cow's milk—we like both, if they're very fresh. After just a few days, ricotta's sweet, lactic taste vanishes, and bitterness creeps in. Buy full-fat ricotta, and search for one that is locally made. Ideally it should be packed in a basket for drainage. The fluffy texture and creaminess of fresh ricotta is unrivaled in desserts; it's the base of our Torta di Ricotta (page 76).

Sometimes we just spread ricotta on toasted bread—during the colder months we shave truffles over ricotta toasts (Bruschetta con Tartufo Nero, page 322), but in spring it's fresh fruit, a drizzle of honey, or a spoonful of Conserva di Rabarbaro (page 74).

Torta di Ricotta

Fluffy ricotta lends its lightness to cheesecake. A spoonful of Conserva di Rabarbaro (page 74) or Marmellata di Kumquat (page 272) over the top is delightful.

....

MAKES ONE 9 INCH/
23 CM CAKE, SERVES EIGHT

1½ pounds/680 grams whole-milk
    ricotta
soft butter for the pan
⅓ cup/40 grams all-purpose flour
    + more for dusting the pan
boiling water for the pan
1 cup/200 grams sugar
1 teaspoon/3 grams salt
1 large lemon
1 pound/454 grams mascarpone
    (or cream cheese), at room
    temperature
2 large eggs + 3 yolks, at room
    temperature
1½ teaspoons/7.5 ml vanilla extract

Wrap the ricotta in a double layer of cheesecloth or set it in a fine-mesh strainer over a bowl until it releases its water, about 1 hour.

Preheat the oven to 325°F/165°C with a rack in the center. Butter the bottom and sides of a 9 inch/23 cm springform pan and dust with flour, then tip upside down and tap out the excess. Wrap the pan snugly with two long pieces of aluminum foil (to do this, make a cross of foil and place the pan on it, then bring up the ends of foil to wrap the pan). Have ready a kettle of boiling water.

Whisk together the flour, sugar, and salt in a small bowl. Finely zest the entire lemon directly into a large bowl, using a microplane zester. Add the ricotta and mascarpone to the bowl and stir gently to blend. Separately, whisk the eggs and yolks with the vanilla and pour them into the bowl gradually, mixing until thoroughly combined. Use a light touch to avoid beating in too much air. Stir in the flour and sugar mixture.

Spoon the batter into the prepared pan and tap the pan firmly on the counter three times, to release air bubbles. Set the pan of cheesecake inside a deep roasting pan and place it on a shelf in the oven. Pour boiling water into the roasting pan to come about halfway up the sides of the springform pan. Bake until the surface of the cake is golden, and a small area in the center of the cake jiggles slightly when you shake the pan, 1¼ to 1½ hours.

Lift the pan out of the water, and transfer to a cooling rack. Remove the foil, and run a knife around the edges of the cake. Let the cake cool at room temperature 1 to 2 hours. Cover the pan and refrigerate for 8 hours, and up to overnight before releasing from the pan.

Fragole e Zabaione

STRAWBERRIES AND SABAYON

The sweetest strawberries served with a pour of lightly sweet, sparkling wine and topped with a dollop of cream—what could be more romantic? Look for a Moscato d'Asti from Piemonte, a little bit sweet, delicate, and fizzy.

....

SERVES FOUR

4 large egg yolks
⅓ cup/65 grams sugar
salt
⅓ cup/80 ml Moscato d'Asti
   + more for serving
8 ounces/225 grams mascarpone
1 pint/250 grams ripe strawberries,
   cut into quarters

Whisk the egg yolks and sugar together in a large glass or metal bowl (a copper bowl is ideal if you have one) until they form thick ribbons that drop from the whisk. Add a tiny pinch of salt and pour in the Moscato. Whisk until the mixture is frothy.

Bring a small pot of water to a simmer. Set the bowl over, but not touching, the water. Whip the egg mixture constantly, incorporating as much air as possible, until it foams and then swells (it will almost double in size), about 5 minutes. Whip until the whisk leaves a deep trace in the zabaione, 1 to 2 minutes more.

Remove the bowl from the heat, set it on a wire rack, and continue whisking for 2 minutes to help it cool down. When cool, fold in the mascarpone, being careful not to deflate the zabaione. Serve over quartered strawberries. Zabaione can be refrigerated for up to 2 days.

2

Summer

It's New York hot. There are the occasional torrential downpours. It's a season of protests and parades and celebrations throughout the city. There's an ongoing hum of regulars at Via Carota seeking sustenance and shade. Some of our guests are visitors to the West Village, having their first taste of a storied enclave that has long embraced musicians, artists, activists, teachers, writers, bakers, bankers—and home to the 1969 Stonewall riots.

There is so much produce coming in that it can be hard for us to keep up. It's the moment to eat food almost untouched, raw. We are serving chilled seafood with capers, and grilled fish, chicken, and vegetables with our lemony salmoriglio. There are sliced tomatoes topped with basil and stacks of fritti for sharing. New York City's local green markets are kitchen therapy, a dose of inspiration. There is nothing like seeing the piles of green beans, the sunflowers, the figs, and the melons in the market.

TOMATOES

THE LONG WAIT

The annual wait for local tomatoes is predictable here in the Northeast. We need a handful of hot days before we can count on juicy tomato salads. Rita will patiently wait until mid-July for tomatoes. Eventually, our local green markets are loaded with a rainbow of heirlooms. Back in the kitchen, where we have tomatoes maturing on a six-foot speed rack, we select only the ripest for the day. The plants keep producing through September, and we are grateful.

JODY & RITA

Insalata di Pomodori

SUMMER HEIRLOOM TOMATO SALAD

At the peak of tomato season, we enjoy this salad daily for weeks, often with burrata. We use a variety of ripe heirloom tomatoes, large and small, which we prize for their mellow sweetness. Never refrigerate your tomatoes—they will lose much of their flavor.

SERVES FOUR

1 spring onion bulb, thinly sliced

8 ripe heirloom tomatoes

1 medium cucumber, peeled

handful fresh basil leaves

extra-virgin olive oil

salt

pepper

Soak the spring onion slices in a bowl of cold water for a minute or two. Drain in a fine-mesh sieve and shake off the excess water; pat them dry with a clean kitchen towel.

Wash, dry, and core the tomatoes. With a sharp knife, slice them into large pieces. Place the tomatoes in a wide bowl, being careful not to lose the juices. Halve the cucumber lengthwise, then cut into pieces of similar size to the tomatoes. Toss the cucumber and onions with the tomatoes.

Stack the basil leaves on top of each other in an orderly way. Roll them up and draw your knife across them to make fine shreds. Add the basil to the chopped tomatoes. Drizzle generously with olive oil and season with salt and pepper. Toss everything together.

Pomodori Verdi con Bottarga

MARINATED GREEN TOMATOES WITH BOTTARGA

Green tomatoes don't need to be pickled or fried; they have a clean, slightly tart flavor and crunchy texture when eaten raw. A plate of thinly sliced green tomatoes with dressing is a quick exercise in layering flavors— basil and lemon add fragrance, while sprinkling bottarga (dried fish roe) on top provides a deep, savory note.

....

SERVES FOUR

2 large green (unripe) tomatoes
 (about 1 pound/454 grams)
salt
extra-virgin olive oil
half a lemon
handful fresh herbs such as
 parsley, basil, mint, chives,
 or celery leaves
piece of bottarga di muggine,
 about 2 ounces/55 grams

Slice the tomatoes into very thin rounds. Use a mandoline if you have one. If not, use a serrated knife or a very sharp chef's knife to make thin slices.

Place about half of the slices on a serving plate. Sprinkle them with salt, drizzle with olive oil, and add a spritz of lemon; toss lightly. Repeat with the remaining tomatoes, sprinkling with salt, drizzling with olive oil, and squeezing lemon over them. Toss the tomatoes with your fingers, creating peaks and valleys on the plate. Tear the herb leaves (but snip the chives, if using). Scatter the herbs over the salad.

Peel off the membrane from the bottarga with a paring knife. Finely grate the bottarga over the salad.

BOTTARGA

Bottarga is sun-dried and salt-cured fish roe, still whole, encased in its natural membrane. It has a uniquely pungent flavor. It might be an acquired taste, but cooks have been enjoying it as a seasoning since antiquity. There are two types available, bottarga di muggine (gray mullet) and bottarga di tonno (tuna).

We prefer muggine. A small amount finely grated or shaved is all you need. It has a powerful, umami finish when sprinkled over salads like the pomodori verdi, simple bowls of pasta with butter, and grilled bread with lemon and olive oil. Any unused bottarga can be stored for months in the refrigerator.

Panzanella

TOMATO BREAD SALAD

There are many uses for days-old bread, and panzanella is one of the best. Chewy, rustic loaves of bread are especially suited to this salad; the juices of tomatoes and a briny soak satisfy the summer palate.

SERVES SIX

½ loaf days-old country bread
3 tablespoons/45 ml aged sherry
    vinegar
salt
1 quart/1 liter water
2 spring onion bulbs
2¼ pounds/1 kg mixed, ripe
    tomatoes
2 small seedless cucumbers,
    such as Persian, or 1 English
    cucumber, peeled
3 celery stalks, thinly sliced
¼ cup + 3 tablespoons/105 ml
    extra-virgin olive oil + more
    for drizzling
large handful fresh basil leaves
pepper
flaky sea salt for sprinkling

Slice or tear the bread into large cubes (about 1½ inch/4 cm), crust included. You should have 5 to 6 cups. Combine the vinegar and 1½ teaspoons/4.5 grams salt in a large bowl and whisk to dissolve the salt. Stir in the water. Soak the bread in the brine until it swells and softens—from 2 to 20 minutes depending on the staleness and density of the bread. Drain in a colander and firmly press out as much liquid as you can without crumbling the bread.

Thinly slice the spring onions and refresh them in a small bowl of cold water, drain, and pat dry. Wash, dry, and core the tomatoes. With a sharp knife, slice the tomatoes into large pieces; halve the cucumbers lengthwise and cut into a similar size. Transfer the tomatoes and their juices and the cucumbers to a large, wide bowl. Toss with the spring onions and the celery, and season with salt (about ½ teaspoon/ 1.5 grams).

Pour a good amount of olive oil (about ¼ cup/60 ml) into the salad, toss in the whole basil leaves, and season with pepper. There will be a lot of juice in the bowl. Add the bread, mixing gently but thoroughly with your hands to coat. Let stand for 5 to 10 minutes and toss again. Use a slotted spoon to lift the panzanella onto plates. Drizzle with olive oil, then sprinkle with flaky sea salt.

TIP · BREAD FOR SALAD

If you have a loaf that is too hard to slice, try wetting
your fingers with water and rubbing the outside of
the bread, then placing it in a 375°F/190°C oven for
10 to 15 minutes to soften it just enough to make it
sliceable. And if you want to make this salad but
don't have day-old bread, you can dry fresh bread
out in the oven. Thickly slice the bread, then tear into
large pieces. Spread in a single layer on a sheet pan.
Drizzle with olive oil and bake at 250°F/120°C until
the edges are dry to the touch, about 30 minutes.
Let the bread cool to room temperature before
using for panzanella.

CUCUMBERS AND MELONS

Cucumbers and melons are cousins, botanically speaking. Once the boundaries between savory and sweet are blurred, it's easy to see how they are almost interchangeable. They share the same thirst-quenching juiciness, and each variety has its own pretty fragrance. We add cucumber to summery tomato salads, spoon it over chilled oysters in a tart mignonette, and juice it into a spritz. As for melon, we serve wedges of ripe cantaloupe with slices of prosciutto, of course. And we plate watermelon with salty olives and feta cheese to emphasize its sweetness. Herb leaves such as basil and mint enhance the scent of both melons and cucumbers.

Bevanda al Cetriolo

CUCUMBER SPRITZ

We opened a little bar called Pisellino across the street from Via Carota in 2019. It's an homage to drinking all things Italian, inspired by our favorite cafés in Florence and Milan. We think that a fresh-squeezed juice and your latte macchiato should feel just as special as an evening cocktail. When we make this nonalcoholic beverage, we make a custom lime cordial for a dash of good old-fashioned bartending.

....

MAKES TWO

1½ large cucumbers, about
    1 pound/454 grams
3 ounces/90 ml Lime Cordial
    (page 94)
4 dashes Saline Solution (about
    ⅛ teaspoon + a few drops)
    (page 94)
1 tablespoon/15 ml lime juice
    (from 1 lime)
ice
sparkling water or seltzer

Slice a few cucumber slices and set aside for garnish. Peel the remaining cucumber and puree it in a blender or run it through a juicer. If blending it, strain the juice, pressing on the solids to extract as much as possible. You should have about ½ cup/120 ml juice.

Stir the lime cordial, saline solution, and lime juice together in a mixing glass (you will have 4 tablespoons/60 ml of this base). Pour in the cucumber juice and stir well.

Fill two highball glasses with ice, pour the cucumber juice mixture into the glasses and top up with sparkling water or seltzer. Garnish with cucumber slices.

LIME CORDIAL

**6 juicy limes (6 ounces/180 ml
  juice)**
1½ cups/300 grams sugar

Peel the limes with a vegetable peeler. Toss the peels with the sugar in a bowl or a large jar. Using the handle of a wooden spoon or a muddler, bruise the peels a little to release their fragrant oils. Cover and leave overnight. The next day, juice the limes directly into the sugar and stir until it dissolves. Lime cordial can be refrigerated up to 2 weeks.

SALINE SOLUTION

A saline solution is a trick many bartenders have up their sleeves. It allows them to add a very tiny amount of salt to a drink in controlled drops. Knowing about balancing flavors is the key to making good drinks: salt accentuates sweetness and tempers bitterness (and vice versa).

2 tablespoons/20 grams salt
**¼ cup + 2 tablespoons/90 ml
  water**

Stir salt and water together until salt dissolves completely. Pour into a small bottle, ideally one with a small opening, or a dropper.

Ostriche

Instead of serving oysters the classic French way—nude with a little ramekin of sauce on the platter—we spoon the sauce into the shells just as they go out into the dining room. The oysters arrive at the table brimming with cucumber and flecks of green basil.

MAKE 2 DOZEN

2 dozen oysters on the half shell
crushed ice
Cucumber Mignonette (page 97)

See our tips (below and page 98) for choosing and opening oysters.

Set the opened oysters on a platter of crushed ice. Spoon cucumber mignonette onto each oyster.

TIP · HOW TO CHOOSE AN OYSTER

When selecting oysters, buy the ones that are raised closest to you. For us, that means between the tip of Long Island and the tip of Cape Cod. Oyster farming is one of the most sustainable types of aquaculture out there, and since oysters are farmed, the old rules about only eating them in months with an R don't matter. Any time of year is good.

CUCUMBER MIGNONETTE

Keep the cucumbers chilled, slice the basil at the last minute, and toss them both into this mignonette sauce before serving.

MAKES ABOUT I CUP, ENOUGH FOR I DOZEN OYSTERS

half a seedless cucumber, such as
    English (4 inches/10 cm)
salt
½ small shallot, very finely
    chopped
I lemon, zested and juiced
2 fresh basil leaves

Peel the cucumber, leaving a few strips of skin on for color. Grate it into a bowl on the medium holes of a grater and season with a pinch of salt.

Rinse the shallots in a fine-mesh strainer with cold water and drain. Stir the shallots into the cucumber. Zest the lemon directly into the bowl and squeeze in the juice (for about I teaspoon zest and 3 tablespoons/45 ml of juice); stir to combine.

Stack the basil leaves on top of each other in an orderly way. Roll them up and draw your knife across them to make fine shreds. Finely chop the ribbons and stir into the mignonette.

To practice your oyster-opening skills, buy more than you need—if, say, you want to eat a dozen oysters, buy two dozen, and forgive yourself if you get crumbled shell on some of them or spill the oyster liquor—soon you'll get the hang of it.

TO CLEAN OYSTERS: We're particular about cleaning our oysters. We scrub them under running cold water with a stiff-bristled brush—a lot of sand and dirt can get trapped in the hinge at the back of each shell. Then we chill them down in a bowl of ice water for about thirty minutes. Keeping them chilled like this helps their shells pop open. As we take them out to open each one, we wipe it down with a damp cloth.

To open an oyster: You'll need an oyster knife. They can be bought from most fish markets and oyster purveyors. Fold a kitchen towel in half and half again, then double it over like a book, or a clam. Place the oyster on the countertop with the flat side up. Grab the towel like a mitt in one hand—the folded part will protect your hand while you work—and the oyster knife in the other. Stick the knife into the hinge of the oyster at about a 45-degree angle and wiggle it with a little bit of force until you feel it notch into place inside the hinge. Press harder and wiggle until you feel the hinge loosen, then give the knife a firm twist to release the shell. When it releases, slide your knife inside the oyster and scrape the top shell to separate it from the oyster. Now you can pop it open. Carefully slide the oyster knife underneath the oyster to sever the muscle from the shell—hold the curved shell firmly so you don't spill the oyster liquor. Scrape off any bits of broken shell. Keep oysters on ice while you open the rest.

REGGIO EMILIA

I arrived in Reggio Emilia to cook with Enzo Bertelli and Alberto Telani at their celebrated Caffè Arti e Mestieri in the late 1980s. My intention was to only stay a month or two, as their aiuta cuoca, kitchen help. Over the next three years, I spent many summer nights with them and the other cooks, eating watermelon and swatting mosquitos. Roadside watermelon stands are a summer tradition. An arrow painted on a wooden board directs you to picnic tables just off the side of the road. Each table holds impressive pyramids of prized watermelons. Those moments were a respite from the kitchen in my Emilia summers.

JODY

Insalata di Cocomero

WATERMELON, RED ONIONS, AND MINT

This savory treatment of watermelon starts a meal or is a nice accompaniment to grilled chicken or seafood.

....

SERVES FOUR

half a small watermelon
½ medium red onion, thinly sliced
　　lengthwise
½ cup/100 grams black olives,
　　such as taggiasca or kalamata,
　　pitted
12 fresh mint leaves
3½ ounces/100 grams feta cheese
2 tablespoons/30 ml Salmoriglio
　　(page 343)

Set the watermelon with the cut side down on a flat surface. Slice it into quarters, then slice off the rounded ends and trim off the rind. Keep the wedges of watermelon flat so they won't slip out from under your knife. Slice into square or rectangular slabs about 2 inches/5 cm thick, and stack them on a plate.

Soak the onion slices in a bowl of cold water for a minute or two. Drain in a fine-mesh sieve, shake off the water, and pat them dry with a clean kitchen towel. Rinse the olives and pat them dry. Scatter the onions, olives, and mint leaves over the watermelon slices. Crumble feta on top and drizzle the salad with salmoriglio.

SEAFOOD

· ·

With summer in full swing, seafood plays a large role on our menu. Crustaceans, bivalves, and whole fish—chilled, grilled, or tossed in a pan.

Insalata Frutti di Mare

CHILLED SEAFOOD WITH SALSA VERDE

A small plate of seafood with a green, capery sauce is a summer starter. Use your best quality extra-virgin olive oil in the salsa verde and for tossing with the seafood.

See notes on cleaning and preparing the seafood below.

. . . .

SERVES FOUR

3 quarts/3 liters strained Court Bouillon (page 349)
ice
½ pound/225 grams calamari or cuttlefish bodies and tentacles
8 jumbo shrimp, shells on
1½ pounds/680 grams mussels
extra-virgin olive oil
salt
3 celery stalks + pale celery leaves
Salsa Verde (page 346) for serving

Bring the court bouillon to a boil in a large pot. Have ready a large bowl of ice water. See instructions below for cleaning and preparing each type of seafood. Poach the seafood, one variety at a time:

- Cook the calamari tentacles (or cuttlefish, if using) in the court bouillon until they're opaque and barely firm—the calamari cook very quickly (30 to 45 seconds). Lift them out of the pot with a spider, and chill in the ice water immediately. Next, cook the calamari bodies just until they're opaque and barely firm, about 30 seconds. (If using cuttlefish, allow 15 to 25 minutes for them to cook.) Transfer to the ice water immediately to cool, then drain them in a colander. Add more ice to the bowl.
- Poach the shrimp until their shells are pink and their flesh is opaque, 2 to 3 minutes. Lift them out of the pot and chill in the ice bath for a few minutes, then transfer to the colander.
- To cook the mussels, pour off most of the court bouillon, leaving about 1 inch/ 2.5 cm in the pot. Return it to a boil, add the mussels, and cover the pot tightly. Steam the mussels open, about 5 minutes; lift out any open mussels. Cover the pot and steam the remaining mussels; discard any that haven't opened at all after 5 more minutes.

Slice the calamari into thin strips. Peel the shrimp; lay them flat and split them in half lengthwise with a sharp knife. Shuck the mussels and discard the shells. Place all the seafood in a bowl and pour in enough olive oil to coat them lightly. Season with salt and toss well. Thinly slice the celery and add to the bowl along with some delicate celery leaves. To serve, arrange the seafood and celery in a single layer and spoon the salsa verde on top.

TO PREPARE THE SEAFOOD FOR POACHING

Slice the cuttlefish or calamari bodies lengthwise and open them flat, like a book. With the side of your knife, scrape off any white or clear membrane. Slice the bodies in half and score a crosshatch pattern on each half.

TO CLEAN AND DEBEARD MUSSELS Set in a colander and rinse them well. Check for any fibers coming from inside the shell—these are called the "beard." Remove the beard by pinching it firmly between your fingers and pulling down. Scrub the mussels well with a firm-bristled brush, and rinse again. Soak mussels in a bowl of ice water for up to 30 minutes, then drain in a colander.

To devein shrimp, cut along the back of the shell with scissors or a paring knife, following the curve of the shrimp. Make an incision running the length of the shrimp. If there is a dark "vein" (the digestive tract) inside the incision, simply pull it off.

LIVING ON A LIRA

Living in Rome, I usually ate at my local forno, pizza al taglio places, rosticcerie, and greenmarkets in Trastevere and Monteverde Vecchio. But, there was a very elegant restaurant behind the Pantheon famous for its spaghetti all'aragosta—a half of lobster with fresh tomatoes and spaghetti. I saved my wages and went there. I devoured this meal of lobster and juicy tomatoes. When you're a young cook, living on a few lire a week, most every meal out is memorable.

JODY

Spaghetti all'Aragosta

LOBSTER, SPAGHETTI, AND CHERRY TOMATOES

A scarlet tangle of spaghetti with lobster is a decadent dinner. It's made from a few ingredients. First: a live lobster.

SERVES FOUR

1 live lobster, about 1½ pounds/
    680 grams
2 quarts/2 liters boiling water
3 tablespoons/45 ml extra-virgin
    olive oil + more for serving
2 large garlic cloves, crushed
dried chili flakes, about
    ¼ teaspoon or to taste
¾ pound/340 grams juicy
    tomatoes such as cherry
small handful fresh basil leaves
salt
½ pound/225 grams spaghetti
2 sprigs fresh flat-leaf parsley,
    coarsely chopped

See directions below for cooking the lobster. Then have the lobster meat ready, cracked and accessible but still in the shell. The lobster's head provides extra flavor to the sauce, so we add it to the pan, but this is optional. Pour the oil into a large skillet and add the garlic and chili flakes; heat over medium until the garlic is fragrant, but not browned (less than 1 minute). Sprinkle the cut sides of the lobster tail, still in its shell, with salt and place in the pan cut sides down (push the garlic to the edges first). Add the lobster head to the pan, if using. Raise the heat to medium-high and add the tomatoes to the pan.

When the tomatoes begin to blister, give the pan a shake. Check the lobster—when the undersides are lightly golden (about 3 minutes), turn them. Add the cracked claws in their shells and any picked lobster meat to the pan. Stir the tomatoes to release their juices and add the basil leaves (about 5 minutes total).

Meanwhile, bring a large pot of water to a boil and add 2 tablespoons of salt. Add the pasta, stirring to prevent it from sticking. Cook until al dente, a minute less than the package instructions.

Reserve about 1 cup/240 ml of the pasta cooking water, then drain the spaghetti. Add the spaghetti to the pan containing the lobster and tomato mixture and pour in ½ cup/120 ml of the pasta liquid; toss the pan while stirring the spaghetti with tongs. The lobster and spaghetti will be tangled, and the tomatoes will break down as you stir them together. Working quickly, stir in the roe, if using, and taste for salt. Add more liquid as needed to create a sauce that lightly coats the spaghetti.

Serve the spaghetti and lobster drizzled with olive oil and sprinkled with parsley. Pass around small forks or lobster picks for the claws.

TIP · FIRST, A LOBSTER

Here's a simple method to kill a lobster: Firmly hold the lobster on the cutting board, belly down. Use the tip of a sharp chef's knife to pierce the lobster behind the eyes; this should kill the lobster instantaneously. Place it in a large bowl, pour boiling water over it, and cover the bowl with a sheet pan or lid for 4 minutes. Lift out the lobster and transfer to a colander until cool enough to handle, about ten minutes.

Split the lobster in half lengthwise: Insert the tip of the knife into the head, then hold it steady while placing firm pressure on the knife handle as you continue down the lobster tail. Separate the halves. Use your fingers to remove the soft, greenish tomalley from below the lobster head and discard it—but if you find any roe along the tail (tiny, black eggs; they turn red when cooked), save them for adding to the sauce.

For cracking and shelling the lobster: Pull off the claws and crack them or cut them open with scissors to make the meat accessible, but keep the meat in the shells. Separate the knuckles and crack them to extract the meat (discard those shells). Separate the tail halves from the head with a firm twist. Keep the tail halves in their shells. Pull off the small legs and, to get the meat out, press on them with the back of a knife, or roll over them with a rolling pin. All of this work can be done ahead of time. The picked and cracked lobster can be refrigerated for up to one day.

SUMMER SQUASHES

We use both green and golden zucchini in summer squash season and take advantage of their blooms, too. Choose squash with shiny, unblemished skin. Small, firm ones are best—they haven't yet developed a fluffy flesh. When they're tender, just slice and serve them raw.

Carpaccio di Zucchine

SHAVED RAW ZUCCHINI, PARMIGIANO,
AND MINT

This salad can be made at a moment's notice. Mix your colors. It's important to layer them thinly on the plate. Choose a larger plate if you are scaling the recipe up. Once again, we urge you to use the best olive oil and parmigiano.

....

SERVES FOUR

5 assorted small/medium summer
   squashes (about 1 pound/
   454 grams)
12 mint leaves
half a lemon
salt
extra-virgin olive oil
piece of Parmigiano Reggiano,
   about 4 ounces/115 grams

Thinly slice the squash into ribbons using a mandoline or a vegetable peeler. Lay the slices flat on a large plate, overlapping slightly. Stack the mint leaves on top of each other in an orderly way. Roll them up and draw your knife across them to make fine shreds.

Squeeze the lemon over the squash (about 1 tablespoon/15 ml of juice), sprinkle with the mint, and season with salt; drizzle lightly with olive oil. Shave parmigiano into large strips with a vegetable peeler and lay them on top of the squash, covering the slices almost entirely. If your plate isn't large enough to accommodate all the slices in a single layer, repeat with another layer of squash, lemon, mint, and olive oil, cover with parmigiano, and finish with a drizzle of olive oil.

Fiori di Zucca

ZUCCHINI FLOWERS FILLED WITH RICOTTA

Zucchini blossoms combine beauty and utility—they're the perfect container for a savory filling. Choose fresh, unblemished petals and use them as quickly as possible after harvesting. Once they are fried, eat them right away while they're still hot and crisp.

MAKES 12

12 zucchini blossoms

TO MAKE THE FILLING

½ cup/120 grams whole-milk ricotta
2 anchovy fillets
2 tablespoons/25 grams Pesto Genovese (page 127)
salt
2 ounces/55 grams mozzarella

TO FRY THE BLOSSOMS

¾ cup/90 grams all-purpose flour
¾ cup/100 grams cornstarch
½ teaspoon/2 grams baking powder
½ teaspoon/1.5 grams salt
sparkling water, about 1½ cups/360 ml
extra-virgin olive oil for frying, about 1½ cups/360 ml
safflower oil for frying, about 1½ cups/360 ml

Slice open each flower and reach inside with a paring knife to trim off the protruding, yellow stamen. Gently clean the flowers with a soft brush. Put the ricotta in a square of cheesecloth or in a fine-mesh sieve and set it over a bowl to drain for 30 minutes, then transfer to a medium bowl. Chop the anchovies and run your knife through them a few more times to make a coarse paste. Stir the anchovies, pesto, and a pinch of salt into the ricotta and mix well. Tear the mozzarella into small pieces and mix it into the ricotta with a fork.

To fill the flowers, use a small spoon, or a pastry bag fitted with a large, plain tip. Spoon or pipe the filling into each blossom until about half full (1 to 2 teaspoons per flower). Press the tips of the petals together to enclose the filling. To make the batter, whisk the flour, cornstarch, baking powder, and salt in a bowl. Pour sparkling water into the flour, whisking as you pour, until combined into a smooth paste the consistency of loose pancake batter.

Pour equal amounts of olive and safflower oil into a straight-sided skillet until about 1 inch/2.5 cm deep (the oil should come halfway up each flower as it cooks). Heat over medium-high heat for about 5 minutes. Test the oil to see if it's ready: drip a little batter into the pot—it should sizzle and float the moment it hits the oil. While the oil is

Fiori di Zucca
continued

heating up, line a sheet pan with a few layers of paper towel and set it next to the stove.

Holding the flowers by the stem end, carefully dip them into the batter one at a time and drop directly into the hot oil. Cook three or four if there is space in the pan, but don't crowd them. Nudge the flowers with a fork or a spider to prevent them from sticking to the bottom of the pot. Cook until golden on the first side, about 2 minutes; turn them over and cook for another minute. Lift out of the pot with tongs or a spider and drain on the paper towels. Sprinkle lightly with salt and repeat with the remaining flowers.

Zucchine Fritte

FRIED ZUCCHINI

A batch of zucchini is one of the least messy things to fry—and great for casual entertaining. Just don't try to be at the table and stove at the same time—wait until you're all done frying to turn off the oil and join the fray.

SERVES FOUR

2 medium zucchini, about
   ¾ pound/340 grams total
¾ cup/90 grams all-purpose flour
¾ cup/100 grams cornstarch
salt
safflower oil for frying, about
   3 cups/720 ml
extra-virgin olive oil for frying,
   about 3 cups/720 ml

Before frying, make sure you are set up, so you can control what's happening in the pot. Cut the zucchini crosswise into 4 inch/10 cm lengths. Slice them into thick matchsticks using a mandoline, or with a knife. Soak the zucchini in a bowl of cold water for 30 minutes.

Sift the flour, cornstarch, and a pinch of salt together into a large bowl. Have ready a sheet pan lined with a few layers of paper towel next to the stove.

Pour both oils into a deep, heavy pot, to come up 3 inches/7.5 cm. Set over high heat. To test the oil to see if it's ready, drop a breadcrumb or a small piece of zucchini into the pot; it should sizzle and float the moment it hits the oil. A candy/deep-fry thermometer clipped on the side of the pot should read 350°F/175°C.

Lift a handful of zucchini out of the water and shake off excess. Working quickly, drop the wet zucchini into the bowl of flour and cornstarch and toss, using your fingers to coat thoroughly. Transfer to a sieve set over the bowl and shake off excess.

Sprinkle the zucchini into the hot oil; they should sizzle immediately. Using a spider or tongs, gently swish the pieces around to stop them from sticking together. Fry until crisp and lightly golden, stirring occasionally,

Zucchine Fritte
continued

about 4 minutes. Transfer from the oil onto the paper towels and sprinkle evenly with salt.

Repeat with the remaining zucchini, adjusting the heat as needed between batches to maintain the temperature. Test the oil before adding each new batch of zucchini. This can be done in four to six batches, depending on the diameter of your pot; don't be tempted to fry more than a handful at once or the zucchini will not become crisp. Pile the fritti high on a plate and serve right away.

SODI FAMILY FRYING

Don't be intimidated by frying. In the Sodi family, we fry food for a party of ten or twenty people. My mother, Elena, chose to fry in the summer—it's the perfect food for eating outside. She would come out of the kitchen carrying enormous plates of fritti: zucchini, onions, green tomatoes, artichokes, rabbit. It varied. The scene at the table was a little bit chaotic, with everybody reaching across to grab something before it cooled.

RITA

EGGPLANT

In late summer, market tables showcase slender
Japanese eggplants and tiny spherical ones, large,
eggshell-white varieties, and the more familiar
deep purple Italian type. Choose what you like.
Large varieties can be bitter, so they will benefit
from salting in advance. You can skip this step
with smaller ones. We like eggplant grilled, with
a drizzle of Salmoriglio (page 343) and as part of
a Verdure alla Griglia (page 148), or slowly cooked
into the Sicilian relish, Caponata (page 122).

Caponata

EGGPLANT, PINE NUTS, CURRANTS, AND CAPERS

You can make this today (or even yesterday) to serve tomorrow, because it is the type of richly layered vegetable dish that improves as the ingredients settle in together. Spoon onto thick slices of grilled bread and serve as part of an antipasto plate.

....

SERVES FOUR

3 medium eggplant
   (1½ pounds/700 grams)
salt
2 tablespoons/15 grams dried
   currants
¼ cup/60 ml warm water
¼ cup/60 ml aged sherry vinegar
   + more for seasoning
extra-virgin olive oil
1 large red onion, finely chopped
2 celery stalks, finely chopped
3 large garlic cloves, finely grated
1 pound/454 grams ripe tomatoes,
   sliced in large pieces
3 tablespoons/45 grams capers,
   rinsed
handful meaty green olives,
   such as castelvetrano,
   pitted and chopped (about
   3 tablespoons/50 grams)
pepper
3 tablespoons/25 grams pine nuts,
   toasted
small handful fresh basil leaves

Slice off the stem end of the eggplants, peel them, and cut into cubes about ¾ inch/2 cm. Set the cubes in a colander and sprinkle with about 1 tablespoon/10 grams salt, tossing to coat them thoroughly. Set the colander over a bowl and press a small plate firmly on top of the eggplant. Drain for 30 minutes to 1 hour with the plate on top. Spread the eggplant out on a clean kitchen towel and pat dry.

Meanwhile, place the currants in a cup and pour the warm water and ¼ cup/60 ml vinegar over them. Set aside until soft and plumped, about 30 minutes; drain.

Heat a large skillet over medium-high and add a generous amount of olive oil (about 3 tablespoons/45 ml); when the oil is shimmering, add eggplant in a single layer (about half of the eggplant). Cook, turning until lightly browned on all sides, 5 to 7 minutes. Transfer to a plate using a slotted spoon. Coat the pan with more oil and repeat, until all the eggplant is browned. Without wiping out the skillet, add the onions, celery, and garlic with a pinch of salt; reduce the heat to medium. Cook until they're soft, stirring often, about 7 minutes.

Return the eggplant to the skillet and stir in the tomatoes, capers, olives, and currants. Cook, stirring occasionally until the tomatoes have completely softened and the caponata has thickened, 20 to 25 minutes. Season with salt and pepper as needed. Stir in the pine nuts, and add vinegar to taste (about 1½ teaspoons/7 ml). Tear the basil and stir into the caponata.

Caponata can be refrigerated up to 5 days; bring to room temperature before serving.

TIP · OLIVE TIPS

We always buy whole olives and pit them ourselves; they're firmer than pitted olives and have a better flavor. But before we do anything with them, we give our olives a dip in cool water and then drain them. Doing this gives them a fresh start and gets rid of some of the saltiness from their brine. Once you have rinsed them you can coat them in olive oil and add seasonings of your choice. We usually add a few sprigs of thyme or rosemary, strips of lemon or orange peel, whole garlic cloves, and sometimes chili peppers.

Try this way of pitting whole olives: Place a few olives on a cutting board and, working one at a time, press down on them with the flat side of a chef's knife. The pressure will split them open, and you can break them apart to pull out the pit. Separate the pits from the flesh.

BASIL

····················

The word *pesto* comes from *pestare*—to pound—
which is the traditional way of making pesto
Genovese. While it's true that the basil leaves
release more of their perfume when pounded by
hand, this is not practical for restaurant cooks
during their busy shifts, so we use a machine. As
a cook in Italy, I learned to make pesto with an
electric meat grinder. It gives the pesto a beautiful,
sandy texture. I liked breaking the parmigiano into
walnut-size pieces and feeding it into the grinder
along with handfuls of pine nuts, watching the
pesto fall slowly into a bowl.

JODY

Pesto Genovese

CLASSIC BASIL PESTO

The best moment to make pesto is mid- to late summer, when basil is at its most aromatic and garlic is being harvested.

MAKES ABOUT 1 CUP/200 GRAMS, SERVES FOUR

3 cups packed/4 handfuls fresh
    basil leaves
1 large garlic clove
salt
¼ cup/40 grams lightly toasted
    pine nuts + more for serving
extra-virgin olive oil + more as
    needed
1 cup/100 grams finely grated
    Parmigiano Reggiano, pecorino
    Romano, or a combination

Wash the basil leaves and dry them well on a clean kitchen towel. Tear the basil into large pieces and remove any thick stems.

Pulse the garlic with a large pinch of salt in a food processor until chopped. Add the basil and pine nuts, with a small pour of olive oil to pulse them into a coarse paste. Scrape down the sides of the bowl and add most of the cheese, reserving a bit. With the machine running, pour in olive oil until the pesto is blended (about ½ cup/120 ml). Add more cheese until it's as creamy as you like and taste the pesto for salt.

If not using pesto immediately, spoon it into a small container and pour a thin layer of olive oil on top to prevent the surface from discoloring. Each time you take some pesto out of the container, drizzle more olive oil on the surface. Pesto can be refrigerated for 3 days.

Trofie al Pesto

HAND-ROLLED PASTA TWISTS WITH BASIL PESTO

Even though this trofie is freshly made, you will cook it for longer than fresh egg pasta (more like dried pasta), so taste a piece to be sure that it's tender but still al dente.

SERVES FOUR

salt

4 portions of Trofie Pasta (page 130)

1 cup/200 grams Pesto Genovese (page 127)

grated Parmigiano Reggiano or pecorino Romano, or a combination, for serving

Bring a large pot of water to a boil and salt it generously (about 2 tablespoons/20 grams).

Cook the trofie in the water until it's al dente, 8 to 10 minutes. Drain it, reserving a cup of pasta water.

Have the pesto ready in a large bowl. Pour in about ¼ cup/60 ml of the pasta water, stirring until smooth. Toss the trofie into the bowl and add a bit more pasta water as needed to create a creamy sauce that coats the pasta. Serve with freshly grated parmigiano or pecorino.

Trofie

HAND-ROLLED PASTA TWISTS

When I make pasta by hand, I like to do it on a wooden board; the surface adds some friction to help you roll. **RITA**

MAKES 4 SERVINGS

all-purpose flour
14 ounces/400 grams Pasta di Semola (page 365)

Have ready a sheet pan dusted with flour and a clean kitchen towel. Divide the dough into four pieces. Work with one piece at a time, keeping the remaining dough covered by a bowl. Pinch off a small piece of dough, about, about the size of a large pea. Roll it briefly between your fingers to make it smooth. Place the ball of dough on the board, and keep your hand flat but tilt it so the base of your thumb sits directly on top of the dough. Press down to roll the pasta, flattening the dough as you slide your hand upward, until the dough is at your wrist.

Lift up your hand and rotate it almost 90 degrees, now placing the *outer* edge of your hand on top of the dough. The dough should be at the bottom of your hand, just above the wrist. Press down firmly while rolling your hand *downward* until the dough reaches the base of your little finger. Lift your hand: the finished piece of pasta will be a short, twirled stick with a tapered end. Set it aside on the board to dry, and pinch off another piece of dough. Repeat, rolling your hand up and down, up and down with each ball of dough.

Allow the rolled trofie to dry on the board while you work with the remaining dough. When your board is full, spread trofie on the floured sheet pan, with a kitchen towel between layers. Air-dry them completely (overnight) if not cooking them right away. Store dried pasta in an airtight container at room temperature.

DOG DAYS OF SUMMER

In the Liguria region, where pesto originated, a vegetable soup, Minestrone alla Genovese (page 133), is often eaten at room temperature during the hottest days. We find the basil-infused broth invigorating. It's a hard sell to American diners, who tend to think of soup only on cold days, but we hope you'll give it a try.

New York can still be swelteringly hot in September, but after a couple of cool mornings in a row and when the evening light starts to dip earlier, we are ready to serve this soup.

JODY & RITA

Minestrone alla Genovese

SUMMER SOUP WITH BASIL PESTO

Here, the peak-of-summer vegetables speak for themselves. The amounts are not exact; adjust to your taste. We make this soup light, without using stock. A batch of pesto can be made in the time it takes for the soup to cook. Once the soup is ready, the pesto is spooned into each bowl, its intoxicating fragrance diffused.

....

SERVES SIX

1 medium red onion, coarsely
   chopped

2 celery stalks, finely sliced

½ fennel bulb (or trimmings),
   diced ½ inch/1.3 cm

2 handfuls green beans or
   yellow wax beans (8 ounces/
   225 grams)

1¾ cups/300 grams cooked beans,
   such as cannellini, drained
   (or 15 ounce/425 gram can)

extra-virgin olive oil

salt

6 cups/1.5 liters water

2 small zucchini, diced ½ inch/
   1.3 cm

3 handfuls baby spinach leaves,
   or other greens

chili flakes

½ cup/100 grams Pesto Genovese
   (page 127)

Combine onions, celery, fennel, and green or yellow beans with the cooked beans in a large pot. Pour in ¼ cup/60 ml oil, 2 teaspoons/ 6 grams salt, and the water. Bring to a boil over high heat and immediately reduce heat to low. Skim off any foam that rises to the surface. After about 2 minutes, add the zucchini.

Cook at a gentle simmer until the onions are translucent and all the vegetables are tender, about 20 minutes. (The vegetables will lose their brightness, but they should not be mushy, and the broth should taste lively.) Stir in the spinach leaves until wilted. Add a pinch of chili flakes, and season with salt as needed. When ready to serve, add a spoonful of pesto to each bowl and drizzle with olive oil.

SUMMER BEANS

Snap, cook, repeat.

Fagiolini Verdi con Pesto

GREEN BEANS WITH BASIL PESTO

Dress green beans while they're still warm; they'll absorb the rich flavors of freshly made pesto.

....

SERVES FOUR

1 pound/454 grams green beans

salt

½ cup/100 grams Pesto Genovese
   (page 127)

1 heaped tablespoon/10 grams pine
   nuts, toasted

Trim the tops from the green beans. Bring a large pot of water to a boil and season it generously with salt (about 2 tablespoons). Cook the beans until bright green and crisp-tender; about 2 minutes. Drain the beans in a colander, shake off any water, then place them in a large bowl. While they're still warm, toss the beans with pesto and sprinkle with toasted pine nuts. Let them sit for a while before serving.

Fagiolini Gialli

BRAISED YELLOW WAX BEANS

Slow cooking reveals the velvety texture of fresh beans—they lose all their snap in a stew of olive oil, tomatoes, and sweet onions. If you'd like to substitute green beans or flat Romano beans, cook them for a little bit longer.

....

SERVES FOUR

1 pound/454 grams yellow wax
    beans, topped and tailed
4 ounces/115 grams sliced
    pancetta, optional
4 tablespoons/60 ml extra-virgin
    olive oil
1 large spring onion or small red
    onion, thinly sliced (1½ cups
    sliced)
2 large garlic cloves, thinly sliced
salt
¾ pound/340 grams ripe plum or
    beefsteak tomatoes, sliced in
    large pieces, juices reserved
1 tablespoon chopped fresh
    rosemary (about 3 sprigs)
1 small dried chili or ¼ teaspoon
    chili flakes

Rinse the beans in a colander. If using pancetta, slice it into lardons about ¾ inch/ 2 cm. Heat the oil in a large skillet over medium heat and add the pancetta and cook until it begins to render its fat, about 3 minutes. Add the onions, garlic, and a pinch of salt. Cook, stirring often, until the onions are tender and almost translucent, 7 to 10 minutes. Add the beans and toss them with the onions until well coated. Stir in the tomatoes and their collected juices, the rosemary, chili or chili flakes, and about ½ teaspoon/1.5 grams of salt.

Cover the skillet and reduce the heat to medium-low. Cook, lifting the lid to stir occasionally, until the beans are very tender, 15 to 20 minutes (the tomatoes will break down into a chunky sauce that coats the beans). Add salt as needed.

Fagioli e Tonno

CANNELLINI AND TUNA

When locally caught albacore tuna is available, we serve it raw in this summery dish. At other times we substitute tuna poached in olive oil, Tonno Sott'Olio (page 356).

SERVES FOUR

½ pound/225 grams sushi-grade albacore tuna

2 teaspoons/10 grams Calabrian chili paste

2 cups/320 grams cooked Cannellini (page 140), drained

2 tablespoons/30 ml Salmoriglio (page 343)

¼ small red onion

10 cherry tomatoes, halved

salt

small handful fresh basil leaves

small handful fresh flat-leaf parsley

extra-virgin olive oil

If using raw tuna, use a very sharp knife to cut it into chunks the size of a small olive. Toss lightly with chili paste; start with a little, adding more to taste. Keep the tuna chilled while you prepare the salad. If using tonno sott'olio, break the tuna into large flakes.

Toss the beans with the salmoriglio. Slice the onion into thin wedges and soak in ice water for 15 minutes. Drain and pat dry. Stir the onions and tomatoes into the beans and season with salt. Add the basil and parsley and gently stir in the tuna. Transfer to a serving plate, finish with a drizzle of olive oil, and serve immediately.

Cannellini

TUSCAN BEANS

Cooked until creamy, and flavored with sage and garlic, these beans are the basis for many dishes, such as Fagioli all'Uccelletto (page 229), Fagioli e Tonno (page 138), and Minestrone alla Genovese (page 133). Adapt the herbs depending on what you have in the kitchen, such as bay leaves or fresh thyme.

....

MAKES 8 CUPS COOKED BEANS,
SERVES SIX

1 pound/454 grams dried cannellini
5 garlic cloves, peeled
1 sprig fresh sage
extra-virgin olive oil
salt

Pour the beans onto a plate and pick through them for any pebbles or small clumps of soil, then place them in a sieve and rinse well. Place the beans in a bowl, cover with about 3 inches/7.5 cm cold water, and soak overnight.

The next day, drain the beans and put them in a pot with enough space for them to double in size. Cover with cold water by about 2 inches/5 cm and add the garlic and sage.

Bring to a boil and skim off any foam that rises to the top. Pour in a generous splash of olive oil (about 2 tablespoons/30 ml). Reduce the heat so the beans are simmering gently, cover the pot, and cook until tender, 40 to 50 minutes. Stir in 1 tablespoon/9 grams of salt and continue cooking gently for 10 minutes. If not using them right away, cool the beans in their liquid, and then refrigerate for up to 5 days, or freeze for up to 3 months.

SUMMER FRUITS

At the end of a summer meal, a plate of fruit, fresh and ripe, is a beautiful moment.

Fichi

SMASHED FIGS WITH SESAME AND HONEY

Keep figs at room temperature and eat them when they feel full and soft.

....

SERVES FOUR

6–8 ripe figs
flavorful wildflower honey
aged balsamic vinegar
1 tablespoon/10 grams sesame
    seeds

Slice the figs in half or tear them with your hands. Arrange them on plates and smash the interiors lightly with a fork. Drizzle with honey and balsamic vinegar. Lightly toast the sesame seeds in a dry skillet over medium heat, shaking the pan until they're aromatic, about 2 minutes. Sprinkle the seeds over the figs.

Macedonia

My mother would eat an apple at the end of each meal. She would always seek to share it with her family, but most of the time everyone said, "No, thank you." Then, my sister, Marzia, made something we all liked: she mixed several fruits together, from peaches to apricot and melon, with lemon juice and sugar. Jody and I always look forward to visiting my sister, and particularly to enjoying her macedonia. **RITA**

....

SERVES FOUR

2 cups/30 grams grapes

1 cup/120 grams blackberries

1 medium melon

2 peaches

1 white nectarine

3 apricots

1 lemon

¼ cup/50 grams sugar

Rinse the grapes and set them aside to drain. Rinse the blackberries, spread them on a kitchen towel, and pat gently to dry. Peel and seed the melon and cut it into small cubes (about 1 inch/2.5 cm). Place the melon in a large bowl.

Rinse the peaches, nectarine, and apricots, and peel them with a paring knife. Dice the peaches, nectarine, and apricot into cubes about the same size as the melon and add to the bowl. Leave the grapes and blackberry whole and stir them in.

Squeeze the lemon over the sugar in a small bowl and stir to dissolve. Pour the lemon sugar over the fruits and stir gently to coat. Leave in the refrigerator for at least 1 hour, up to 4 hours. Mix thoroughly before serving.

Pesche al Forno

ROASTED PEACHES IN AMARETTO

At the peak of summer, the racks in our kitchen are loaded with peaches at varying stages of ripeness. We get a hit of their perfume every time we walk by. Choose the ripest you can find for this—when they're sweet and juicy you won't need to add any sugar.

SERVES FOUR

4 ripe peaches
2 tablespoons/25 grams sugar,
    if needed
¼ cup/60 ml almond liqueur
vanilla ice cream or mascarpone
    for serving

Preheat the broiler with a baking pan in it. Cut the peaches into quarters and arrange them, cut side up, on the hot pan. If the peaches aren't very sweet, sprinkle them lightly with sugar.

Sprinkle the liqueur over the peaches (about 1 tablespoon/15 ml per peach). Broil until the fruit is blistered in places and the juices are released, about 10 minutes. Slide the peaches onto a plate and scoop mascarpone or ice cream on top.

3

Grilling

Grilling over fire requires complete focus: you're in constant motion, turning ingredients when they're charred and sizzling, and moving others to a cooler spot to finish cooking. You have to be vigilant, watching closely to avoid burning anything. Live fire also provides flexibility, giving you different temperature zones to work with. It's a dynamic way to cook.

Grilling over a fire adds unique flavor. Still, we use the gas grill in the restaurant kitchen every day for grilling seasonal vegetables—and the house favorite, grilled chicken with salmoriglio. But what fun to be outdoors on a hot summer night! When we're on vacation, we take advantage of any grilling opportunity. After a grilled meal, we make use of the cooling coals, adding beets or whole onions in their skins to let them roast slowly to use the next day. We then sit and watch the fading embers.

JODY & RITA

Verdure alla Griglia

GRILLED VEGETABLES

A main course? For us, yes.

SERVES SIX

3 medium red onions

6 bell peppers

2 medium eggplants

2 medium zucchinis

6 spring onions, with greens

24 whole shishito peppers,
  about ¾ pound/340 grams

12 whole small tomatoes on the
  vine or 24 cherry tomatoes

1 large head romaine lettuce or
  escarole

1 loaf country bread, cut in thick
  slices

extra-virgin olive oil

salt

1½ cups/355 ml Salmoriglio
  (page 343)

1 large garlic clove

handful fresh basil leaves

Slice all the vegetables into thick slices or wedges (except the spring onions, shishito peppers, and tomatoes, which will be grilled whole). Cut the lettuce or escarole into thick wedges through the core. Wash them in two changes of cool water, and drain them in a colander, shaking off the water. Brush both sides of the sliced bread with olive oil and sprinkle with salt.

Set up a grill with two temperature zones: high and indirect heat (or very low). Indirect heat is an area of the grill you can place anything that's already cooked or needs to finish cooking slowly. To do this, if using a large charcoal grill, build two piles of coal at different heights, banking them gradually. The highest one will be the hottest, and the low one, with just one layer of coals, will be used for indirect cooking. If using a large gas grill, set the heat to medium, and the shelf above the grill will be your indirect zone (or set one portion of the grill to low). If using a grill pan, cook the vegetables in batches over high heat, and keep each cooked batch in a warm place while the rest is cooking.

Grill the vegetables in batches, beginning with the ones that take longest to cook. Toss the vegetables lightly with olive oil and salt before grilling. Grilling times are as follows:

- **RED ONIONS** Cook until charred on all sides and move to indirect heat to finish cooking until tender (about 15 minutes total)
- **BELL PEPPERS** Cook until lightly charred and move to indirect heat to finish cooking until softened (about 15 minutes total).
- **EGGPLANT** Cook until deeply browned on each side and move to indirect heat to finish cooking, until the center is very soft when pressed (10 to 12 minutes total).
- **ZUCCHINI** Brown on each side and cook until barely tender (about 6 minutes total).
- **LETTUCE OR ESCAROLE** Cook until wilted (6 to 8 minutes total).
- **SPRING ONIONS** Lay flat and grill until lightly charred; when the greens have wilted, fold them up over the bulbs to stop from blackening (5 to 7 minutes total).
- **SHISHITO PEPPERS** Cook whole, turning until blistered and blackened (about 5 minutes total).
- **TOMATOES ON THE VINE OR CHERRY TOMATOES** Cook whole, turning as they burst and blacken (about 5 minutes total).

Arrange the vegetables on a platter and spoon salmoriglio over them. Grill the bread on both sides until lightly charred. Cut the garlic clove in half and rub it on both sides of the hot bread. Scatter basil leaves over the vegetables just before serving.

TIP · SETTING UP FOR GRILLING

It's important to have everything set up and organized before you begin grilling. Have olive oil and salt next to the grill and a platter ready to put everything on when it's finished cooking. Scrub your grill clean and wipe it with an oiled rag just before grilling anything that might stick to the grates, like delicate seafood or vegetables.

Keep seafood chilled right up until the moment you are ready to throw it on the grill—at the restaurant we set up a pan of ice next to the grill for this purpose. Stay alert so you don't overcook anything, taking each item off as soon as it's done—every mussel, every shrimp. Vegetables are much more forgiving. Avoid charring them but don't undercook them, either—they must be tender. Taste as you go to check. The secret is to cook in stages, beginning with the things that take longer.

Bamboo skewers are a useful tool for grilling smaller items, from shishito peppers and scallops to batons of swordfish. Threading them onto skewers keeps them from falling through the grates, and allows you to turn a few pieces at the same time— important when the fire is hot, and everything is cooking quickly. Soak bamboo skewers in water for at least 20 minutes before grilling to prevent the wood from burning on the grill.

Grigliato Misto di Pesce

GRILLED SEAFOOD

This is ideal for eating with a group. There is a variety of seafood to taste and share. Have plenty of napkins and a bowl for shells on the table.

SERVES SIX

1–1½ pounds/454–680 grams swordfish steaks

1½ cups/355 ml Salmoriglio (page 343)

18 large sea scallops, about 1 pound/454 grams

1½ pounds/680 grams jumbo shrimp, shells on, or 12 large spot prawns

¾ pound/340 grams calamari

1½ pounds/680 grams mussels or littleneck clams

ice

6 spring onions

12 whole small tomatoes on the vine or 24 cherry tomatoes

extra-virgin olive oil for grilling

salt

1 loaf of country bread

2 lemons

Soak 12 bamboo skewers in water for at least 20 minutes. Meanwhile, cut the swordfish into batons (about 1 x 3 inches/2.5 x 7.5 cm). Thread them onto skewers (2 to 3 per skewer), place them flat on a tray, and pour enough salmoriglio over them to coat lightly (about ¼ cup/60 ml), tossing to coat. Pat the scallops dry and score a crosshatch pattern on both sides. Thread them onto skewers. Place the skewers flat on the tray; pour enough salmoriglio over them and toss to coat lightly (about 2 tablespoons/30 ml). Devein the shrimp, and clean and score the calamari (page 106). Toss the shrimp and calamari in separate bowls with enough salmoriglio to coat them lightly (about 2 tablespoons/30 ml each). Reserve the remaining salmoriglio. Scrub and debeard the mussels (page 106) or scrub the clams and set them on ice.

SET UP THE GRILL

Set up a grill with three temperature zones: high, medium, and indirect heat (or very low). Indirect heat is an area of the grill on which you can place anything that's already cooked or needs to cook slowly. To do this, if using a large charcoal grill, build three piles of coal at different heights, banking them gradually. The highest one will be the hottest, and the lowest one, with just one layer of coals, will be used for indirect cooking. If using a large gas grill, set half of the grill to high and the other half to medium—the shelf above the grill will be your indirect zone. If using a grill pan, cook the seafood in small batches over high heat, and keep each cooked batch in a warm place while the rest is cooking.

USE THE MEDIUM HEAT ZONE FOR THE VEGETABLES, AND THE MUSSELS OR CLAMS:

- Brush the spring onions and tomatoes with oil, and sprinkle with salt. Grill them over medium heat: Lay the onions flat and grill until lightly charred; when the greens have wilted, fold them up over the bulbs to stop them from blackening, and move to indirect heat, 5 to 7 minutes total. Grill the tomatoes until they're beginning to soften, about 3 minutes, then move to indirect heat.
- Cook mussels or clams over medium heat, spreading them flat on the grill. As soon as their shells open (3 to 4 minutes), they're done. Pick them up carefully to keep any juice inside the shells, and place them, shell and all, in a large bowl. Spoon salmoriglio over them. (Allow up to 5 more minutes for any shells that haven't opened—but discard them after that.)

USE THE HOTTEST PART OF THE GRILL FOR THE SWORDFISH, SCALLOPS, SHRIMP, CALAMARI, AND BREAD:

- Lift the swordfish skewers out of the marinade, letting any excess drip off, and sprinkle the swordfish with salt. Brush the grill with oil just before grilling. Grill them without moving, until marked by the grill, 2 to 3 minutes; flip the skewers and cook for about 2 minutes more. The fish is done when the edges are opaque and the center is still slightly soft when pressed.
- Brush the grill with oil just before grilling the scallops. Salt them lightly and brush with oil.

Grill them without moving until marked by the grill, about 2 minutes. Flip them with a metal spatula and grill them until just cooked in the center, 1 to 2 minutes more.

· Salt the shrimp and grill them over high heat until the shells are pink, about 2 minutes, then move them to medium heat to finish cooking until the flesh is opaque, 1 to 2 more minutes. Set on a pan over indirect heat. Brush the grill with oil and grill the calamari on both sides until marked by the grill; pull them off as soon as they are opaque, about 2 minutes total.

· Brush the bread with oil and grill both sides until marked by the grill, then set on a pan over indirect heat.

Arrange everything on a platter. Quarter the lemons. Spoon a little bit of salmoriglio over everything and pour the rest into a small bowl for the table.

FREESTYLE

We keep an open mind when grilling fish and seafood, and you should too—the rules are few. Use what is fresh. If swordfish isn't available and another fish is enticing, buy that instead. Other meaty steaks of fish, like tuna, halibut, and mahi mahi, grill easily; or try fillets of fish with the skin on, such as salmon, bass, and bluefish, and small, whole fish like sardines. Avoid delicate white fish. Grill softshell crabs when in season, and wild shrimp or spot prawns with their heads on.

JODY & RITA

Pollo alla Griglia

GRILLED CHICKEN IN SALMORIGLIO

Here nothing distracts from the straightforward appeal of chicken grilled over a fire. The chicken is briefly marinaded in our lemony salmoriglio. But first, we brine it, just as we do with all our white meats. A savory brine seasons chicken to the bone and keeps it juicy, too. However, if you don't have time to brine, just give the chicken a turn in the marinade before putting it on the grill.

A small chicken serves two to four people. Since halves are easier to manage on the grill than a whole bird, we recommend grilling two halves at the same time. You can also adapt this for a whole, spatchcocked chicken.

....

SERVES TWO TO FOUR

2 half chickens or 1 whole chicken,
   2¾–3 pounds/1.3–1.4 kg total
10 cups/2.5 liters Brine (page 350)
1½ cups/360 ml Salmoriglio
   (page 343)
1 lemon, cut in ¼ inch/6 mm
   rounds
flaky sea salt

If beginning with a whole chicken, cut the chicken in half using kitchen shears or a strong, sharp knife. Remove the backbone and reserve it for making chicken stock.

Submerge the chicken in brine in a deep container. Cover and refrigerate for 2 to 3 days. Remove the chicken from brine, pat dry, and transfer to a dish large enough to hold it flat. Pour about ½ cup/120 ml salmoriglio onto each chicken half; turn the chicken to coat. Marinate at room temperature for at least 30 minutes, and up to 2 hours.

Preheat a grill to medium, with a lower heat zone for indirect cooking. If using charcoal, bank the coals, with a lower pile of coals to one side; if cooking on a gas grill, turn two sections of the grill to medium heat and one section to low. (It's always useful to have an indirect zone, an area of the grill where you can place anything that needs to cook slowly or is already cooked.)

Wipe the marinade off the chicken and place the chicken on the grill skin side up. Discard the used marinade. Grill chicken for 10 minutes on each side, flipping as the skin and underside brown, and moving it around as needed to avoid flare-ups. Reduce the heat to low (or move the chicken to indirect heat), flip the chicken so it's skin side up, and cover the grill. Cook until the juices of the thigh run clear with no trace of pink when pierced, about 20 minutes, or more for a larger chicken. A thermometer inserted in the thickest part of the thigh should read 165°F/75°C. Flip again, if needed, to crisp and brown the skin.

Transfer the chicken to a cutting board to rest for 10 minutes. While the chicken is resting, dip the lemon slices in the remaining salmoriglio and grill them on both sides until lightly charred.

Spoon salmoriglio over the chicken, sprinkle it lightly with salt, and serve with the grilled lemon.

Note: If you don't have an outdoor grill, you can roast the chicken. Preheat the oven to 425°F/220°C and roast the chicken on a sheet pan without turning, for about 45 minutes. Roast or broil the lemon slices while the chicken is resting.

Rosticiana alla Griglia

GRILLED PORK RIBS WITH BLACK PLUMS

Look for ribs with a good amount of meat on them. We roast the ribs until tender, then give them a blast on the grill and toss with grilled plums and sweet onions.

SERVES FOUR

3–3½ pounds/1.4–1.5 kg meaty spareribs, such as St. Louis style

salt

pepper

extra-virgin olive oil

2 red onions

4 ripe black plums

6 sprigs fresh rosemary

about 1 teaspoon/5 ml aged sherry vinegar

water as needed, about ¼ cup/ 60 ml

Season the pork ribs all over with salt and pepper and let stand at room temperature for least 30 minutes, up to 4 hours. Rub them with olive oil and wrap them snugly in two layers of aluminum foil and place on a sheet pan.

Preheat the oven to 425°F/220°C and roast the ribs for 20 minutes. Reduce the oven temperature to 325°F/165°C and cook until the ribs are thoroughly tender, and juice is collecting in the foil, about 1½ hours (unwrap them to check after 1 hour and 15 minutes). Open the foil to let the ribs cool to room temperature. At this point you can grill them right away or re-wrap the room temperature ribs and refrigerate them overnight. Bring them to room temperature before grilling the next day.

Preheat a grill to medium-high. Meanwhile, peel and slice the onions into thick rings (about ½ inch/1–2 cm) and halve the plums. Place a large, heavy skillet directly on the grill (or on the stovetop over medium-high). Coat with olive oil (about 2 tablespoons/30 ml) and add the onions, rosemary, and a pinch of salt. Cook the onions on both sides until browned, about 10 minutes. While they're cooking, brush the plums with oil and grill on the cut side until they're lightly browned. Add the plums to the pan with the onions. Cover the grill. When plums have released their juices and softened (about 10 minutes), add vinegar to taste (¾–1 teaspoon/3–5 ml), and water if the pan seems dry (about ¼ cup/60 ml). Remove the pan from the heat.

Unwrap the ribs, pour the collected juices into the skillet, and stir to combine. Place ribs on the grill and brown until lightly charred and crisp on both sides, moving as needed to avoid flare-ups, 5 to 10 minutes total. Slice between the bones and place the ribs in the skillet to toss with the sauce. Serve with the onions and plums poured over the ribs.

NOTE Without a grill, you can brown the ribs under the broiler or in a grill pan or for 10 minutes while cooking the onions and plums in a skillet on the stovetop.

4

Aperitivi

The aperitivo hour is an opportunity to meet friends, hear the latest news, and unwind over a quick drink.

At our bar, Pisellino, on the corner of Grove Street and Seventh Avenue, we serve drinks made with herbal amari and vermouths, as well as custom nonalcoholic drinks—stirred or spritzed. Then, there is something savory or salty, like hand-cut potato chips and salami with pecorino—e di più (and even more). This is a good pause in the day.

MASTER THE NEGRONI

Everyone should learn to master a spritz and a negroni. A few essential bottles like Campari, Aperol, Cocchi Americano Bianco, gin, red vermouth, and prosecco, and a mixing glass with a bartender's long-handled spoon, are all you need. (Use Cynar instead of Campari if you are in an earthy mood.) Jody prefers vermouth, specifically Vergano Bianco, with soda and a double lemon twist, but I am a negroni fan. I have made many variations on this classic; at I Sodi, we have had a lengthy and unique negroni list for more than ten years. Stir the negroni in a mixing glass with ice. Then pour your chilled drink into a glass with ice. Squeeze an orange peel over the negroni before dropping it in. Enjoy. **RITA**

Negroni Classico

This is by far the most popular drink at our bar.

....

MAKES 2

3 ounces/90 ml Beefeater gin

3 ounces Antica Formula vermouth

3 ounces/90 ml Campari

2 orange wedges

Stir the gin, vermouth, and Campari with ice in a tumbler or mixing glass. Strain into chilled rocks glasses filled with large ice cubes. Drop an orange wedge into each glass.

Negroni Bianco

....

MAKES 2

3 ounces/90 ml gin, such as
  Beefeater

3 ounces/90 ml Cocchi Americano
  Bianco

1 ounce/30 ml amaro, such as
  Amara d'Arancia or Amaro
  Nonino

2 orange twists

Stir gin, Cocchi, and amaro with ice in a tumbler or mixing glass. Strain into chilled rocks glasses filled with large ice cubes. Squeeze an orange peel twist over each drink and then drop into each glass.

Sbagliato

Prosecco instead of gin gives this negroni its name: sbagliato (a mistake, or messed-up). We keep a custom sweet vermouth mix at the bar made up of 50/50 Punt e Mes and red vermouth, and we use it in this drink.

Stir Campari, Punt e Mes, and vermouth with ice in a tumbler or mixing glass. Strain into two chilled rocks glasses filled with large ice cubes. Drop an orange twist into each glass and top up with prosecco.

....

MAKES 2

3 ounces/90 ml Campari

1½ ounces/45 ml Punt e Mes

1½ ounces/45 ml red vermouth

2 orange twists

3 ounces/90 ml prosecco

SALATINI

....

Bar Pisellino sits directly across from Via Carota.
Every morning, the staff sets up café tables on the
sidewalk, where locals sip their espressos and eat
small pastries from our pasticceria menu. Pisellino
has no kitchen; each batch of tramezzini, arancini,
and stuffed ascolana olives is made in the Via
Carota kitchen. The cooks crisscross narrow Grove
Street in their clogs and aprons carrying trays of
food for the bar.

Arancini

RICE FRITTERS WITH 'NDUJA

MAKES 24 ARANCINI

6 cups/1.5 liters water

extra virgin olive oil

2 shallots, finely chopped

1½ cups/300 grams risotto rice,
    such as nano vialone

½ cup/120 ml dry white wine

salt

1 large egg yolk, lightly beaten

2 cups/200 grams finely grated
    Parmigiano Reggiano + more
    for serving

5 ounces/140 grams Monterey
    Jack cheese, medium grated
    (about 1¼ cup)

⅓ cup/75 grams 'nduja

FOR FRYING

1½ cups/180 grams all-purpose
    flour

2 large eggs

2 cups/100 grams fine
    breadcrumbs

safflower oil for frying, about
    3 cups/720 ml

extra-virgin olive oil for frying,
    about 3 cups/720 ml

Bring the water to a bare simmer in a medium pot. Coat a wide, heavy saucepan with oil (about 3 tablespoons/45 ml), set over medium heat, and cook the shallots until soft, 2 to 3 minutes, then add the rice. Using a wooden spoon, stir constantly until the grains of rice are glossy and well coated, about 2 minutes. Raise the heat to medium-high and pour in the wine, stirring until evaporated.

Add 2 teaspoons/6 grams salt to the pot of water. One ladleful at a time, add hot water to the rice, and stir until it's completely absorbed. Continue adding hot water gradually, only adding more when the rice is ready to absorb it (you will know it's ready when the bubbling increases and the spoon leaves a slow trail in the rice). Stir after each addition of water and cook until the risotto is loose and creamy and when you bite into a grain of rice it's barely tender, 18 to 20 minutes (you may have up to 1 cup/240 ml of water left). Quickly stir in the egg yolk, and then the parmigiano and Monterey Jack. Add salt as needed. Spread the risotto onto a sheet pan to cool as quickly as possible.

The risotto can be made ahead up to this point and refrigerated, tightly wrapped, for up to 1 day.

FORM INTO ARANCINI Roll about 3 tablespoon/55 grams of the risotto into ovals about 2½ inches/6.5 cm between slightly damp hands. Pinch off a piece of 'nduja about the size of a chickpea (½ teaspoon/4 grams) and stuff it into the center of each ball, pressing the risotto around the 'nduja to enclose it completely.

Before frying, set up three bowls for dredging the arancini: pour flour into one bowl, and eggs into another; lightly beat the eggs. Place breadcrumbs in the third bowl. Working a few at a time, roll the arancini lightly in the flour, then eggs, and then in breadcrumbs, shaking off the excess at each step. Place a paper towel–lined tray next to the stove.

Combine both oils in a deep, heavy pot (the oil should be 3 to 4 inches/7.5 to 10 cm deep), and heat until hot enough that a breadcrumb sizzles the moment it hits the oil (350°F/175°C on a candy/deep-fry thermometer). Fry the arancini in batches of six, turning to cook until golden brown all over, 3 to 4 minutes. Lift them out of the oil with a spider and roll them on paper towels. Sprinkle hot arancini with grated parmigiano.

Olive all'Ascolana

FRIED SAUSAGE-STUFFED GREEN OLIVES

We transform the traditional sausage-stuffed olives by also adding a layer of sausage on the outside, almost like a tiny Scotch egg. This makes them a substantial snack, or spuntino. It's great to have some ready in the freezer for an aperitivo (if frozen, defrost them in the refrigerator before frying).

MAKES ABOUT 48

8 sweet Italian sausages (1½ pounds/680 grams)
4 large eggs
½ cup (1.5 ounce/50 grams) finely grated Parmigiano Reggiano + more for serving
½ cup (1.5 ounce/50 grams) finely grated pecorino Romano
1 cup/240 ml whole milk
3 cups (300 grams) plain breadcrumbs (or torn white bread)
1 pound/454 grams pitted, large green olives in brine, such as ascolana
all-purpose flour, as needed
safflower oil for frying, about 3 cups/720 ml
extra-virgin olive oil for frying, about 3 cups/720 ml

Slice the sausages open lengthwise and remove the meat from the casings. Crumble it into a large bowl. Lightly beat 1 egg and add to the sausage, then stir in the parmigiano and pecorino. In a separate bowl, pour the milk into 1 cup/100 grams of breadcrumbs and let sit until the breadcrumbs have absorbed all the milk. Squeeze out any excess milk and add the soft breadcrumbs to the sausage. Mix thoroughly with your hands.

Drain the pitted olives from their brine, rinse thoroughly, and pat them dry. For each olive, take a small pinch of filling and stuff it inside the cavity. Use a spoonful of the mixture to coat the olive, pressing the olive in the palm of your hand to completely encase it in sausage. When all the olives are filled and coated, you can refrigerate them up to 1 day before breading and frying them.

Set up three bowls for breading: Pour flour into one bowl, the remaining 3 eggs, lightly beaten, into another, and the remaining breadcrumbs into a third bowl. Working in batches of about 8 olives, roll each olive lightly in the flour, then eggs, and then in breadcrumbs, pressing so they adhere. At this point the olives can be refrigerated for up to 2 days or frozen for 1 month—bring to room temperature before frying.

FOR FRYING Combine both oils in a deep, heavy pot until 3 to 4 inches/7.5 to 10 cm deep and set over high heat. Test the oil to see if it's ready; if you drop a breadcrumb into the pot it should sizzle and float the moment it hits the oil. A candy/deep-fry thermometer clipped on the side of the pot should read 350°F/175°C. While the oil is heating up, line a sheet pan with a few layers of paper towel and set it next to the stove.

Fry the breaded olives in batches, turning until golden brown all over, 3 to 4 minutes. Lift them out of the oil and drain briefly on the paper towels. Dust with parmigiano just before serving.

Coccoli

FRIED BREAD WITH PROSCIUTTO

These mini rolls each hold a bite of prosciutto. We adapted them from a Florentine street food, to serve with aperitivi at the bar.

....

MAKES 24 ROLLS

**half batch Schiacciata dough
(page 177) or 10 ounces/
280 grams of pizza dough
all-purpose flour for rolling
safflower oil for frying, about
3 cups/720 ml
extra-virgin olive oil for frying,
about 3 cups/720 ml
flaky sea salt
½ pound/225 grams thinly
sliced prosciutto**

Gently pull the dough into an oblong shape and slice it into three even pieces. Slice each of those pieces into eight (they will weigh about ¾ ounce/20 grams each) and cover them with a kitchen towel. Flour your hands and roll each piece into a ball (about the size of a ping-pong ball).

Combine both oils in a deep, heavy pot until 3 to 4 inches/7.5 to 10 cm deep and set over high heat. Test the oil to see if it's ready; if you drop a tiny piece of dough into the oil it should sizzle and float the moment it hits the oil. A candy/deep-fry thermometer clipped on the side of the pot should read 350°F/175°C. While the oil is heating up, line a sheet pan with a few layers of paper towel and set it next to the stove.

Fry one ball of dough in the oil to check that it is cooked on the inside before frying the rest. Turn the ball frequently until deep golden all over, about 3 minutes. Lift out of the oil with a spider, drain briefly on the paper towels, and sprinkle with salt. Fry the coccoli in batches, making sure not to crowd them. Split the rolls open while still warm and stuff each one with a slice of prosciutto.

Schiacciata all'Olio

OLIVE OIL FOCCACIA

Schiacciata is Tuscan slang for focaccia. Making naturally leavened bread is a time-consuming process—and it's worth it. It begins with the starter (la madre). Once you are in the habit of feeding a starter regularly, making dough is a natural progression. And your schiacciata will follow. You'll need several hours to start the process—mixing and stretching the dough. We feed our madre and the levain (the raising agent for your dough) with a mixture of half whole wheat and half bread flour. See our tips on page 181.

NOTE: *We weigh ingredients with a scale and use metric measurements; it makes understanding ratios easy. This is helpful when making bread dough, so we are putting metric measurements first.*

....

MAKES 1 SHEET OF FLATBREAD
(18 X 13 INCH/46 CM X 33 CM)

FOR THE LEVAIN

30 grams/about 3 tablespoons recently fed
   La Madre (page 181)
35 grams/about 2 tablespoons + 1 teaspoon
   warm water (about 80°F/27°C)
35 grams/about 3 tablespoons flour
   (half whole wheat and half bread flour)

The night before you want to make the schiacciata, make the levain: Stir the starter and water together in a glass jar until the starter has dissolved. Add the flours and mix until there are no lumps. Cover loosely and leave at room temperature overnight. The next day, when the levain is bubbly and has almost doubled in size, it is ready for baking.

350 grams/about 1 ½ cups warm
water (about 80°F/27°C)
100 grams/¼–⅓ cup Levain
(page 177)
330 grams/about 2⅓ cups bread
flour
120 grams/about 1 heaped cup
whole wheat flour
9 grams/about 1 tablespoon salt
extra-virgin olive oil
flaky sea salt

FOR THE DOUGH

The day you want to make the schiacciata, combine the levain and water in a large bowl and mix to dissolve the levain. Stir in the flours with your hands to incorporate into a shaggy dough; don't try to make it smooth at this point. Scrape the sides of the bowl clean, cover with a kitchen towel, and leave for 30 to 45 minutes.

After the dough has rested, sprinkle the 9 grams/1 tablespoon salt over the surface. Wet your fingers and poke the salt into the dough. Work the dough, pressing it through your fingertips and kneading it a little bit until the salt is dissolved and the dough feels smooth—it does not need to make a neat ball at this point.

Cover the bowl with a kitchen towel with a lid on top and set it in a warm place. This begins the bulk fermentation period. The total bulk fermentation time is approximately 3½ hours, with a few minutes needed every 30 minutes for pulling the dough.

After 30 minutes, make the first pull: Wet one hand and reach underneath the dough to lift it up, then fold it over itself completely. Rotate the bowl 90 degrees, pulling the dough over itself at each turn, for a total of four rotations (360 degrees). Cover the bowl and return to a warm spot in the kitchen. Repeat the pulling and turning every 30 minutes for the first 2½ hours. You will notice that the dough becomes smoother and stretchier between pulls. Make firm pulls, stretching it each time. After 2½ to 3 hours the dough will be fuller and softer. Now, make gentle pulls to avoid deflating any air bubbles that are building up in the dough. After about 3½ hours, the dough should be light and billowy, with large air bubbles trapped inside.

Coat a sheet pan with olive oil (about 2 tablespoons/30 ml). Gently drop the dough onto the pan and stretch it to fill about ¾ of the pan. If it won't stretch, let the dough rest, covered with a kitchen towel, for another 20 minutes and try again. It will not fill the pan completely; uneven edges are fine. Cover the dough and let it rest for 45 minutes.

Preheat the oven to 425°F/220°C. Poke dimples all over the surface of the dough with your fingers and drizzle olive oil over it. Sprinkle with flaky sea salt. Bake until golden brown on top, about 25 minutes.

....

TIP · STARTER SUCCESS

For a good chance of success when creating a starter, here are a few tips: keep it in a place where the air temperature is stable and protected from cold drafts, such as inside a kitchen cabinet or on top of the refrigerator. Stir it well each time you feed it to help the bacteria thrive. Only feed the starter with unbleached flour. To begin a starter, use whole wheat or dark rye, but for subsequent feedings you can combine the whole wheat or rye with bread flour, 50/50. It's helpful to keep a container of mixed flours on hand for regular feedings.

TIP · WORKING WITH TIME
AND TEMPERATURE

The temperature of the environment greatly affects
the activation of your levain and the fermentation
time of your dough. They will come to life much more
quickly in a warm room; conversely, if the room is
cold it could take a few hours longer. Keep checking
and be patient.

Adjust the baking process to your own schedule;
you can slow down the fermentation and chill the
dough overnight for baking the following morning.
After stretching the dough onto the pan, cover with
a kitchen towel and wrap in plastic—refrigerate for
several hours, up to overnight. This allows you to
postpone baking the schiacciata. Bring the dough
to room temperature 1 hour before baking. This
will yield a schiacciata with a more pronounced
sourdough flavor.

....

TIP · MAKING YOUR OWN
SOURDOUGH STARTER

If you aren't able to get a little bit of a friend's starter
you can often buy sourdough starter from a bakery
or a baking supply shop. If you'd like to create your
own starter, it's simple to do; you will combine flour
and water and replace some of the mixture with fresh
flour and water at regular intervals until lively enough
to leaven a dough. The whole process can take from
5 to 14 days. Be consistent and patient; eventually it
will be active and bubbly enough to use for baking.
Once you have an active starter, you can keep it
healthy and strong by feeding it regularly. Feed it
every day if you bake often. Or you can store it in
the refrigerator and feed it every week or two- when
you want to bake with the starter, bring it to room
temperature and feed it twice a day for 2 to 3 days to
strengthen it. This way it will last for years.

La Madre

SOURDOUGH STARTER

whole wheat flour or dark rye flour
warm water (about 80°F/23°C)
bread flour

Combine equal weights of whole wheat or dark rye flour and warm water. We recommend starting with 60 grams of each (about ½ cup flour and ⅓ cup warm water). Combine them in a clear container with space for the mixture to double, and stir well with your hand to dissolve any lumps of flour. Loosely cover the container with a lid and set it in a warm place. Leave it until small bubbles are visible on the surface, one to three days.

Now the culture is activated. If it develops a skin on top, remove it, and give your starter a feeding. Each day at approximately the same time, take out a third of the starter and mix it with equal amounts of flour and water. Discard the remaining starter from the day before (or save to use in recipes that call for sourdough starter discard) and replace it with the newly fed starter. Stir it well.

Continue feeding, replacing a portion of the old with the new mixture daily. After three to five days your starter will have a fruity and yeasty smell. At that point, you can begin using a combination of bread flour and whole wheat flour (50/50). When your starter is bubbling actively and rising each day, make a Levain (page 177) and begin baking with it.

LITTLE SANDWICHES

We serve an assortment of classic finger sandwiches at Bar Pisellino, inspired by the elegant bars of Florence and Milan.

Note: Use high-quality sandwich bread such as pain de mie, Japanese milk bread, or brioche, crusts trimmed. Slice each sandwich into three rectangles to make finger sandwiches. Provide an assortment—make enough so each person gets to taste two of each style.

Tramezzini al Tonno

LITTLE SANDWICHES WITH TUNA, CAPERS, AND OLIVES

If you have a batch of Salmoriglio (page 343) on hand, stir in a spoonful or two before seasoning with lemon juice.

MAKES 6 SANDWICHES

1 cup/225 grams Tonno Sott'olio (page 356)
quarter of a red onion, finely chopped
2 tablespoons/30 grams capers, rinsed and chopped
3 tablespoons/50 grams pitted and chopped meaty green olives, such as castelvetrano
2–3 tablespoons/30–45 grams mayonnaise
2–3 tablespoons/30–45 ml fresh lemon juice
1 tablespoon finely chopped fresh flat-leaf parsley
salt

Lift tuna out of the oil, letting most of the oil drain back into the jar. Place the tuna in a medium bowl, and flake it with a fork. Place the onions in a strainer and rinse with cold water. Drain and pat dry. Add the onions to the tuna. Stir in the capers and olives, and add mayonnaise and lemon juice to taste. Stir in parsley, and a good pinch of salt.

Tramezzini di Pollo

LITTLE SANDWICHES WITH CHICKEN, WALNUTS,
AND CURRANTS

*Poaching chicken is a simple way
to prepare it for salad. To season
when poaching, add celery
trimmings and any fresh herbs
you have on hand.*

MAKES 6 SANDWICHES

1¼ pounds/570 grams bone-in
   chicken thighs

salt

4 stems fresh herbs, such as thyme
   or parsley

1 celery stalk

2 tablespoons/15 grams dried
   currants

2 tablespoons/30 ml aged sherry
   vinegar

2 tablespoons/30 ml warm water

2 tablespoons/15 grams walnut
   pieces, toasted

1 small apple, finely diced

mayonnaise

2–3 tablespoons/30–45 ml Via
   Carota Vinaigrette (page 340)

pepper

Place the chicken in a large pan and cover with 1 inch/2.5 cm cold water. Add 1 teaspoon/3 grams of salt, and the herb stems. Add half the celery stalk to the pot, reserving the other half. Bring to a boil, then reduce the heat to medium-low and cook at a bare simmer until chicken is no longer pink near the bone, about 25 minutes. Remove from water and let cool on a plate. Meanwhile, soak the currants in a small bowl with the sherry vinegar and 2 tablespoons/30 ml warm water until soft, about 30 minutes. Finely dice the reserved celery.

When the chicken is cool enough to handle, pull the meat off the bone, and cut into small pieces. Mix the chicken with the celery, walnuts, and apple. Drain the currants and add them to the bowl. Stir in mayonnaise and vinaigrette to taste (about 2 tablespoons/30 ml) and season with salt and pepper.

Tramezzini all'Uovo

LITTLE SANDWICHES WITH CURRIED EGG SALAD

MAKES 6 SANDWICHES

8 large eggs

ice water

⅓ cup/80 grams mayonnaise, or
to taste

3 teaspoons/9 grams curry powder

3 tablespoons finely chopped
chives

salt

Place eggs in a pot and cover with cold water. Bring to a boil and immediately turn off the heat. Set a timer for 8 minutes.

Prepare a medium bowl of ice water and as soon as the timer goes off, scoop out the eggs and drop them into the water. Let cool for a few minutes—if the water becomes warm, refresh with cold water. Crack the shells and return eggs to the water for a minute before peeling.

Peel and finely chop the eggs and transfer them to a medium bowl. Gently stir in the mayonnaise, curry powder, and chives, and season with salt as needed.

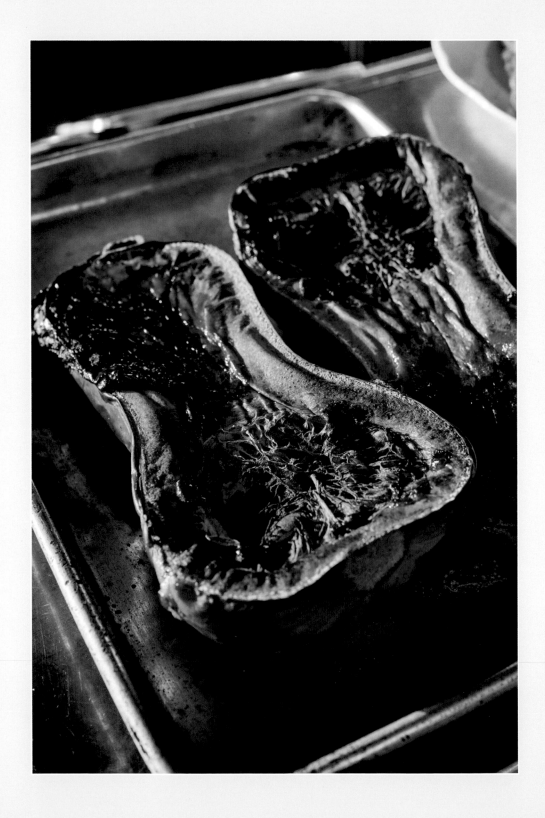

5

Autumn

When September arrives, we start to plan the fall menu, taking into account the last of the summer figs and the final batch of fresh basil pesto. Soon we will be shelling beans, putting up tomatoes, brining and conserving meats. We brush off large porcini mushrooms, just arrived, before thinly slicing them for salads. We roast amber squash in their skins and toast earthy grains and nuts. We are stirring giant pots of onions, Swiss chard, and kale, and simmering robust sauces for pastas for hours. We await the delivery of new harvest olive oil from Italy, stocking our shelves with the emerald-green cans.

MUSHROOMS

....

Deliveries of freshly picked porcini, maitake,
and other fungi bring the scent of the forest
directly to our kitchen.

Sottobosco

SHAVED PORCINI, WALNUTS, AND DRIED
BLUEBERRIES

*Sottobosco, "under the woods"—
when wild mushrooms, thyme,
nuts, and inky berries come
together on the plate.*

SERVES FOUR

2 large or 3 medium firm
    porcini mushrooms (about
    6 ounces/170 grams total)
6 sprigs fresh thyme
¼ cup/35 grams dried,
    unsweetened blueberries
¼ cup/60 ml aged sherry vinegar
¼ cup/60 ml hot water
salt
3 tablespoons/45 ml Dried Porcini
    Vinaigrette (page 342)
piece of Parmigiano Reggiano,
    about 3 ounces/85 grams
¼ cup/30 grams toasted and
    chopped walnuts

Carefully clean the mushroom caps and
stems using a soft brush or damp kitchen
towel. Trim the base of each stem with a
paring knife, peeling off any exterior soil;
once cleaned, wrap the mushrooms in a dry
kitchen towel while you make the salad.

Strip the thyme leaves off the stems, reserving
the leaves. Place the blueberries in a small
bowl with the thyme stems and vinegar and
pour the hot water over them. Cover and let
stand until the blueberries are plump, about
30 minutes.

Very thinly slice the mushrooms lengthwise
through the cap and stem, using a mandoline
or a sharp knife. Arrange the mushroom
slices in a single layer on a large plate,
sprinkle with salt, and spoon about half
of the vinaigrette and half the thyme leaves
over them.

Shave the parmigiano into strips with a
vegetable peeler and lay them on top of the
mushrooms. Scatter half of the walnuts
and the blueberries over the cheese. Repeat
with another layer of mushrooms, salt,
cheese, walnuts, blueberries, and thyme.
Drizzle with a little bit of the liquid in which
the blueberries steeped. Spoon porcini
vinaigrette lightly over the salad.

Funghi alla Griglia

GRILLED MAITAKE MUSHROOMS WITH SMOKED
SCAMORZA CHEESE

*At Via Carota, we use an
assortment of mushrooms—king,
enoki, oyster—cooked in clusters
on the hot plancha until golden
brown. At home, a griddle or a
large skillet made from cast iron
will give you the same intense
heat. We choose scamorza cheese
for the way it melts, and we like
the subtly smoked variety.*

SERVES TWO

12 ounces/340 grams mixed
    mushrooms, such as: 1 king
    mushroom and 4 clusters
    of maitakes, shimeji (beech
    mushrooms), or oyster
    mushrooms
extra-virgin olive oil
salt
4 thick slices smoked scamorza
    cheese
Fennel Seed Salt (page 357)
¼ cup/60 ml Dried Porcini
    Vinaigrette (page 342)

Carefully clean the mushrooms; use a soft
brush or damp kitchen towel to wipe the
caps and stems. Trim the base of clustered
mushrooms where they are woody or dirty.
For king mushrooms, keep the stem long,
slice the mushroom in half lengthwise, and
score the stem a few times.

Heat a well-seasoned griddle or large cast-
iron skillet over medium-high and lightly
coat with oil (about 1 tablespoon). Cook
the mushrooms in a single layer, pressing
down on them as they sizzle, to brown as
much surface area as possible. Don't crowd
the pan; cook in two batches if necessary.
Sprinkle with salt and continue cooking
until golden brown on both sides, about
8 minutes total. Turn off the heat and let
the mushrooms rest on the griddle to soften;
tent with foil to keep them warm.

Meanwhile, preheat the broiler. Place the
cheese slices in a single layer on a sheet pan
and broil until melted, golden brown, and
blistered, about 3 minutes. Use a spatula to
slide the cheese onto a warm plate and lay
the mushrooms on top. Sprinkle lightly with
fennel seed salt and spoon 3 to 4 tablespoons
of porcini vinaigrette over them.

SQUASH

In Emilia-Romagna, where I cooked for three years, zucche, the large pumpkins with hard green skin, are sold whole or in wedges so you can see their deep orange flesh. We often use butternut squash for our risotto. Consider roasting a squash whole; it's already in the perfect container and it's much easier than peeling and chopping it raw. And when cooked in its skin, the sweetness of a squash is intensified. Since the ovens are usually on in our kitchen, it's easy for us to pop a squash into a hot oven before we start prepping a dish like risotto—but you can roast yours in advance and bring it to room temperature before you want to cook with it.

JODY

Zucca in Agrodolce

SQUASH MARINATED WITH ONIONS AND
CURRANTS

Any number of squash varieties are well suited for this uniquely Venetian marinade. Butternut is sweet and silky in texture, while red kuri has dense flesh and a subtle chestnut flavor with an edible skin. Arrange in a single layer so the marinade and spices flavor every slice.

SERVES FOUR

1 small butternut or red kuri
    squash (1¼ pounds/570 grams)
extra-virgin olive oil
salt
1 medium red onion, thinly sliced
    (about 1 cup sliced)
2 dried bay leaves
1 cinnamon stick
½ cup/120 ml aged sherry vinegar
½ cup/120 ml water
¼ cup/about 30 grams currants
1 tablespoon/12 grams sugar
3 tablespoons/30 grams pine nuts,
    lightly toasted

Preheat the oven to 400°F/200°C. Cut the squash in half lengthwise. Rub the squash halves all over with olive oil, salt them well, and set on a baking pan. Roast until the squash halves are blistered in places and soft, 35 to 40 minutes. When cool enough to handle, scrape out the seeds with a spoon.

Place a medium skillet over medium-low heat and lightly coat the bottom with olive oil (about 1 tablespoon). Add the onions, bay leaf, and cinnamon stick. Cook until the onions are beginning to soften, about 5 minutes. Stir in the vinegar, water, currants, sugar, and 1 ½ teaspoons/4 grams salt. Raise the heat to medium-high and simmer until the liquid is reduced by half, 2 to 3 minutes. Turn off the heat and stir in the pine nuts. Slice the squash about 2 inches/5 cm thick and arrange on a platter.

Spoon the marinade over the squash, distributing onions, currants, and pine nuts over the slices. Let stand for at least 15 minutes, or refrigerate for up to 24 hours. Consider making this ahead of time to let the flavors mingle. Serve at room temperature.

Risotto Zucca e Radicchio

SQUASH RISOTTO WITH RADICCHIO

Every time I add white wine to a pan of rice and the puff of steam hits my face, the aroma sends me back to Reggio Emilia, learning how to make risotto. Sixteen bubbles together on the surface, they told me, and you know it's ready to add the butter. **JODY**

SERVES FOUR

1 medium butternut squash
   (1½ pounds/680 grams)
extra-virgin olive oil
1 large shallot
1 cup/100 grams finely grated
   Parmigiano Reggiano + more
   for serving
6 cups/1.5 liters Vegetable Broth
   (page 348), or water
1½ cups/300 grams risotto rice,
   such as nano vialone
salt
½ cup/120 ml dry white wine
4 large leaves of radicchio
6 tablespoons/85 grams cold
   butter cut into pieces

Preheat the oven to 400°F/200°C. Rub the squash with olive oil, set it on a baking pan, and roast until completely soft, 45 to 50 minutes. When cool enough to handle, slice it open and scrape out and discard the seeds. Finely chop the shallot and grate the parmigiano.

Bring the stock or water to a bare simmer in a small pot. Coat a wide, heavy saucepan with oil (about 3 tablespoons/45 ml) and cook the shallots over medium heat until soft, then add the rice. Using a wooden spoon, stir constantly until the grains of rice are well coated, about 2 minutes. Raise the heat to high and pour in the wine, stirring until evaporated. Add 1½ teaspoons/4.5 grams salt to the pot of stock.

Scoop some roasted squash directly into the pan (about two spoonfuls per person; ¾ cup/185 grams total); it will soften into the rice. Reduce the heat to medium. One ladleful (about ½ cup/120 ml) at a time, add hot stock to the rice, and stir until it's completely absorbed. Continue adding hot stock one ladleful at a time, only adding more when the rice is ready to absorb it; you will know it's ready when the bubbling increases and the spoon leaves a slow trail in the rice. Stir after each addition and cook until the risotto is loose and creamy and a grain of rice is barely tender, 18 to 20 minutes. (You may have up to 1 cup of stock left in the pot.) Before the last ladle of stock, tear the radicchio leaves into large pieces and stir them into the risotto. Turn off the heat and work pieces of cold butter into the risotto, stirring rapidly as it melts. Stir in the parmigiano, and add salt as needed. Spoon the risotto onto warmed plates and sprinkle with more parmigiano.

TIP · RISOTTO RULES

A wooden spoon is always used for stirring risotto because it will not break the grains. One of the first steps is to cook the rice in hot butter or olive oil until each grain is coated, but sometimes we take that rule a bit further, and stir the rice in the pan long enough that it smells a little bit toasted.

The sign of a good risotto is in its loose texture; the rice should be lightly bound together yet each grain distinct, tender with a firm bite. When it's the right consistency, risotto will move like a slow wave (all'onda). This comes from the starch in the rice being released by vigorous stirring, and from steady additions of hot liquid. Risotto needs enough liquid to create this movement, so use your judgment when adding each new ladleful.

CABBAGES

·····················

Cabbage and its cousins bring freshness to the fall table. Thinly slice large cabbage as you would for slaw. Buy Brussels sprouts on the stalk. It's fun to snap each sprout off. Then pull off the leaves one by one, and treat them like the little cabbages that they are—toss them in a crunchy salad.

Insalata di Cavoletti

BRUSSELS SPROUTS SALAD WITH WALNUTS
AND APPLES

Try a strong, cave-aged cheese like castelmagno or pecorino di fossa crumbled into this crunchy salad, or even a clothbound cheddar, aged for at least three years.

SERVES FOUR

¾ pound/340 grams Brussels
    sprouts

salt

½ cup/120 ml Via Carota
    Vinaigrette (page 340)

piece of aged cheese such as
    castelmagno, about 3 ounces/
    85 grams

¾ cup/75 grams walnut pieces,
    toasted

2 sweet red apples, such as Gala

1 orange

3 tablespoons pomegranate
    seeds (from about a quarter
    pomegranate)

Rinse the Brussels sprouts and discard any wilted outer leaves. Use a paring knife to trim the base of each sprout. Gather any nice leaves that fall while trimming and pull off as many more as you can; when you get to the hard center of each sprout, slice it thinly with a sharp knife. Put all the leaves and slices in a large bowl with a large pinch of salt and 5 tablespoons of vinaigrette, tossing and working the vinaigrette into the Brussels sprouts with your fingers.

Use the tip of the paring knife or the tines of a fork to crumble the cheese into small pieces, and add them to the salad, along with the walnuts. Slice the apple into thick matchsticks and add half of them to the salad. Finely zest the orange directly over the bowl, then toss everything together. Let the salad settle for about 10 minutes. Add more vinaigrette and salt to taste and pile the remaining sliced apple and the pomegranate seeds on top.

Cavolo e Farro

GREEN CABBAGE AND TOASTED FARRO
WITH SPECK

We begin by toasting farro in the oven, and then simmering it with rosemary, layering in flavors and textures, as we like to do.

....

SERVES FOUR

2/3 cup/about 125 grams pearled
   or semi-pearled farro
3 cups/720 ml cold water
salt
1 large sprig fresh rosemary
extra-virgin olive oil
½ medium green cabbage
   (¾ pound/300 grams)
2–3 tablespoons/30–45 ml Via
   Carota Vinaigrette (page 340)
piece of Parmigiano Reggiano,
   about 2 ounces/55 grams
6 thin slices speck or prosciutto

Preheat the oven to 375°F/190°C. Spread the farro on a rimmed sheet pan and roast until it's lightly browned and smells toasted— about 10 minutes. Spoon the farro into a medium saucepan and add the water, 1½ teaspoons salt, the rosemary, and a generous drizzle of olive oil (about 1 tablespoon). Bring to a boil over high heat. Stir, and reduce the heat to simmer the farro gently until it's barely tender (not quite al dente), 10 to 12 minutes. Drain in a colander, shake off any water, and spread the farro onto a lightly oiled sheet pan. Stir to coat farro with the oil and set aside until completely cool.

Halve the wedge of cabbage and slice it finely, to make about 4 cups. Toss the cabbage in a large bowl with a large pinch of salt and 2 tablespoons vinaigrette, working the dressing into the cabbage with your hands. Add the farro and toss it well. Shave the parmigiano into the bowl with a vegetable peeler, and add more vinaigrette and salt as needed. Pile the salad high on plates and drape slices of speck or prosciutto over the top.

Farro is an ancient form of wheat. When it's toasted, its nutty and earthy flavors reveal themselves. Whenever we cook farro, we add a toasting step before cooking it in liquid. It's important not to overcook the grains; they should be soft at the edges but still have a nice bite. So we spread the farro out to cool after it has come off the stove.

Most often, farro will be pearled or semi-pearled already—the Italian packages often say perlato. This means that the bran has been removed, and the grain has been polished. Unpearled farro is less common, and takes a long time to cook.

LEEKS AND ONIONS

These are the sweetness at the bottom of every
pot and they're staples in our kitchen. Rita grew
up eating dishes made with red onions, and they
remain her favorite for cooking.

Porri al Cenere

CHARRED LEEKS WITH SHEEP'S MILK CHEESE

The outer layer of these leeks is thoroughly blackened, and the insides are steamed until soft and creamy. If you don't have a grill or a stovetop grill pan, you can char them over the flames on your stovetop; in that case, hold one leek at a time with tongs and turn it carefully until blackened all over. Be sure to turn off your smoke detector first.

....

SERVES FOUR

4 large leeks

salt

extra-virgin olive oil

about 3 tablespoons/45 ml water

3 tablespoons/45 ml Via Carota
    Vinaigrette (page 340)

2 ounces/55 grams mild sheep's
    milk feta

Trim the leeks about an inch above the point at which they turn green and begin to fork. Cut into 5 to 6 inch/13 to 15 cm lengths.

To wash them, peel off the outer layer, and soak the leeks twice in a bowl of warm water; lift out after each soak and repeat with new water. Follow with a cold rinse, checking the ends for any remaining soil; drain and pat dry.

Preheat a grill or a grill pan over medium heat. At the same time, preheat the oven to 400°F/200°C. Grill the leeks, turning occasionally, until their surface is completely blackened, about 20 minutes.

Place a large sheet of parchment or newspaper on a sheet pan and arrange the leeks in the center. Season the leeks with salt and a drizzle of olive oil, and sprinkle with water. Fold the paper over the leeks to create a sealed packet, tucking the ends underneath to keep it from opening. Place the pan in the oven until leeks are very soft when pressed (or test with the tip of a knife), about 30 minutes.

Open the packet to cool slightly. Make a lengthwise slit down the middle of each leek. Press the ends to open each leek a bit. Season the interior lightly with salt and a little vinaigrette and crumble cheese on top.

CHARRED LEEKS

Our menu is inspired by many places. You could say we gather stories as much as we do recipes. We were inspired by the Catalan ritual of cooking spring onions in a fire and wrapping them in newspaper to steam, and we have seen whole onions fire-roasted at a market in southern Italy. The newspaper is used to rub away the burned outer layer, and it keeps the onions warm.

In a restaurant kitchen, you must adapt your dreams into a reality that can be repeated efficiently, over and over during service. So for our leeks, we char the outsides first and then steam them in a parcel in the oven.

JODY & RITA

Carabaccia

ONION AND BREAD SOUP

An elemental version of onion soup, carabaccia is quite light, as it's made without meat broth. An egg cracked into each bowl makes this a simple supper.

....

SERVES FOUR

2 pounds/about 1 kg red onions

2 medium carrots

2 celery stalks

extra-virgin olive oil

4 fresh sage leaves

salt

pepper

7 cups/1.75 liters Vegetable Broth
   (page 348)

1 cup/240 ml hot water, or as
   needed

4 thick slices country bread

4 large eggs

¾ cup/75 grams finely grated
   Parmigiano Reggiano, for
   serving

Halve the onions lengthwise and thinly slice the halves. Finely dice the carrots and celery. Coat the bottom of a large, heavy-bottomed pot with olive oil (about 2 tablespoons/ 30 ml) and set over medium heat. Add the onions, carrots, and celery and the sage leaves; stir in 1½ teaspoons/4 grams salt and a few grinds of pepper. Reduce the heat to medium-low and cook gently, stirring often, until the vegetables are completely soft and begin to release their sweetness, 30 to 40 minutes. When the onions begin sticking to the bottom of the pot, raise the heat to medium-high, pour in the stock, and bring to a simmer.

Stir the soup, partly cover the pot, and reduce the heat to medium. Cook until the soup is a deep, tawny color and the olive oil has risen to the top, about 45 minutes; season with salt and pepper as needed. The soup should be brothy—add hot water to thin it if necessary.

Toast the bread and place a slice in each soup bowl. Ladle soup on top and carefully crack 1 egg into each bowl and stir to break it; the egg will cook softly in the hot soup. Drizzle each bowl with olive oil and sprinkle with an abundant amount of parmigiano.

Tortelli di Ricotta Affumicata

SMOKED RICOTTA TORTELLI WITH RED ONIONS

Caramelized red onions and smoked ricotta is a harmonious combination.

MAKES ABOUT 48 TORTELLI, SERVES FOUR TO SIX

all-purpose flour or semolina

12 ounces/340 grams Pasta Sfoglia (page 363)

Smoked Ricotta Filling (page 216)

⅓ cup/100 grams Confettura di Cipolla (page 217)

12 tablespoons/170 grams cold unsalted butter, in thick slices

pepper

1 cup/100 grams finely grated pecorino Romano + more for serving

TO ROLL THE PASTA Have ready a sheet pan lightly dusted with flour or semolina and a pasta drying rack. Have a few clean kitchen towels on hand. It's useful to have a pasta roller, but a sharp knife will do. Divide the pasta dough into 4 portions. Work with one portion at a time and keep the remaining portions covered with a bowl to prevent them from drying out as you work.

Flatten one portion of dough with the heel of your hand until it's about ½ inch/1.5 cm thick. Feed it once through the widest setting (#1) of the pasta roller. Fold the dough into thirds and rotate it 90 degrees to pass the narrow side of the rectangle through setting #1 again. Repeat a couple of times until the dough is smooth and even. Adjust the roller to the next setting (#2) and pass the dough through it twice. Feed through each subsequent setting one time until it's thin enough to see the shadow of your hand. Cut the dough into 4 lengths. Lay them flat on the pan, and cover with a kitchen towel. Repeat, keeping the rolled pasta sheets covered while you work.

TO FORM THE TORTELLI Have ready a second pan dusted with flour. Working with one sheet of dough at a time, lay pasta on a lightly floured work surface and cut across in intervals as wide as the pasta sheet (about 5 inches/12 cm) to make squares (each pasta sheet will make 10 to 12 squares). Place a rounded teaspoon of filling in the center of each square. One square at a time, dip your finger in water and rub it lightly along the edges. Bring two opposite corners of the square together to create a triangle, enclosing the filling in the crease. Use your fingertips to compress the dough around the filling, eliminating any air pockets. Press the edges of the pasta together to seal them. Now you have a half-filled triangle. With the pasta triangle lying flat, bring the two points from the longest side of the triangle together and press them together tightly. The tortelli should look a little like plump hearts. The finished tortelli will be flat on the bottom with a single point on one side, like a folded bandana. Place the tortelli in a single layer on the flour-dusted pan and cover them with a kitchen towel to keep from drying while you roll the next portions of dough. Continue filling and folding tortelli, separating the finished layers with kitchen towels so they don't stick together.

If not cooking right away, dust with flour and tightly wrap the tray with plastic. Tortelli can be refrigerated for up to 24 hours.

TO COOK AND SERVE TORTELLI Bring a large pot of salted water to a boil and cook half the tortelli (or cook in smaller batches), stirring gently to prevent them from sticking together. Cook until the thickest corner of pasta is tender but still slightly al dente, 3 to 4 minutes.

While the tortelli are cooking, heat the confettura di cipolla in a large sauté pan over medium heat. Add half of the butter to the onions and chill the rest in the refrigerator. Scoop out about ¾ cup/180 ml of pasta water and add it to the onions; bring the mixture to a simmer. Add the cooked tortelli to the pan; stir to coat them with the buttery onions. Cook the rest of the tortelli and add them to the pan. Stir in the remaining butter and add more pasta water (about ¼ cup/60 ml) to the pan as it melts, stirring to make a silky sauce. Season with plenty of pepper and gently stir in the pecorino. Serve tortelli with a dusting of pecorino.

SMOKED RICOTTA FILLING

If you can't find smoked ricotta, we provide a recipe for making your own on page 358. You can also use plain ricotta mixed with parmigiano to fill the pasta.

....

MAKES ABOUT 2 CUPS/600
GRAMS, ENOUGH FOR 48
TORTELLI

¾ cup/180 grams smoked ricotta
   (page 358)
1 cup/100 grams finely grated
   Parmigiano Reggiano
1½ cups/360 grams mascarpone
¾ teaspoon/2 grams salt

Stir all the ingredients together in a bowl and refrigerate until ready to make the tortelli.

CONFETTURA DI CIPOLLA: RED ONION JAM

Slow cooking brings out the natural sweetness of onions.

....

MAKES ABOUT ½ CUP/150 GRAMS

1 pound/454 grams red onions
extra-virgin olive oil
salt

Halve the onions lengthwise and thinly slice them in half-moons. Heat a medium skillet over medium-high heat and generously coat with oil (about 3 tablespoons/45 ml). Add the onions and cook until sizzling, about 5 minutes. Add salt (about ½ teaspoon/1½ grams), and stir the onions well. Reduce the heat to medium-low and cook, stirring often, until the onions are very soft and begin sticking to the bottom of the pan, about 25 minutes more. Season with salt as needed.

THE CHAPEL CHAIRS

Via Carota is made up of humble objects. There is the long, old oak table in the center of the dining room where roasted pears and crostata cool. We fold the menu into the backs of beechwood chapel chairs we brought back from the kitchen in Via del Carota. We then found eighty more to match, in an antique shop outside of London.

At heart, we are collectors, spending hours looking for old ash baskets for holding cloth napkins, large earthenware crocks for the sheets of stiff, white paper to cover the tables, and vintage floral plates for desserts. Jody says all the good things find us. Our home fills up with our finds: stools, baskets, crocks.

Brown and earthy hues are beautiful, like an onion slowly caramelizing, or farro with borlotti beans. Objects with character add warmth to the room. Textures and surfaces are subdued, and the lighting is soft, because the energy is kinetic when the place is packed.

Where's the cash register? Hidden in a handmade basket to mask the glowing screen.

The outside world should not intrude when you are at the table.

JODY & RITA

LEGUMES AND BEANS

The autumn larder includes legumes and dried beans. Dishes made with these staples suit the season, satisfying us as we come in from the cold.

Farro e Borlotti

SPELT, CRANBERRY BEANS, AND SMOKED
PANCETTA

For this hearty side dish, we cook farro like risotto, toasting it first in fat and then adding water in two batches. The pork is a seasoning—we use whatever smoky or salty scraps of cured pork we have on hand, which is usually pancetta, a hock of prosciutto, or a piece of guanciale—but thick-cut bacon or leftover ham would work too. If using bacon, cook a couple of extra slices for serving on top.

MAKES ABOUT 8 CUPS,
SERVES SIX

**piece of pancetta, guanciale,
   prosciutto, or ham, about
   4 ounces/115 grams**
extra-virgin olive oil
2 sprigs fresh rosemary
2 cups/375 grams pearled farro
3½ cups/840 ml water
salt
**3 cups cooked borlotti beans in
   their liquid (page 224)**

Dice the pancetta (or other pork product, if using) into pieces about ¾ inch/2 cm. Coat the bottom of a medium saucepan with olive oil (1–2 tablespoons/15–30 ml) and add the pancetta, or other cured pork. Cook over medium heat until the pancetta is sizzling and golden brown at the edges, 4 to 5 minutes. Add the rosemary and the farro, stirring to coat them thoroughly with the fat until the farro smells toasted, about 5 more minutes.

Meanwhile, bring the water to a simmer and add 1 teaspoon salt. Pour half of the water into the saucepan—it will make a loud noise and bubble actively. Cook, stirring frequently, until the water has been absorbed, 5 minutes. Stir in the remaining water and cook, stirring, until the farro is glossy and just tender, about 20 minutes. Use a slotted spoon to add the beans to the skillet. Stir in enough of the bean-cooking liquid to give the farro and beans a little sauce. Heat until bubbling slowly, about 5 minutes. Serve drizzled with olive oil.

Borlotti

CRANBERRY BEANS

We think of borlotti for the fall menu. In September, heaping piles of the marbled red pods can be found at farmer's markets. Later in the season, when they are dried to a muted brown, we rely on them even more.

....

MAKES 3 CUPS OF BEANS

1¼ cups/about 225 grams dried
    cranberry beans (borlotti)
8 garlic cloves, lightly crushed
extra-virgin olive oil
salt

Pour the beans onto a plate and pick through them for any pebbles or clumps of soil, then place them in a sieve and rinse well. Place the beans in a bowl, cover with about 3 inches/ 7 cm cold water, and soak overnight.

The next day, drain the beans and place them in a pot with enough space for them to double in size. Cover with cold water by about 1 inch/2.5 cm and add the garlic. Bring to a boil and skim off any foam that rises to the top. Pour in a generous splash of olive oil (about 2 tablespoons/30 ml). Reduce the heat so beans are simmering gently, cover the pot, and cook until tender, 30 to 45 minutes. Stir in salt (about 1½ teaspoons/4.5 grams) and simmer gently, uncovered, for 10 minutes. If not using them right away, cool the beans in their liquid and refrigerate for up to 5 days, or freeze for up to 3 months.

Lenticchie con Cavolo Nero

BRAISED LENTILS AND KALE

The small brown lentils grown in Tuscany and Umbria can cook long enough to absorb the flavors of the pot without breaking down. Serve a bowl of these lentils hot, with a drizzle of olive oil on top.

SERVES FOUR

1⅓ cups/265 grams small lentils, such as Castelluccio, or French le Puy

1 onion

1 celery stalk

1 medium carrot

4 large leaves lacinato kale

extra-virgin olive oil

1 garlic clove, crushed

1 fresh sage leaf

1 cup finely diced pancetta or guanciale (about 4 ounces/ 115 grams)

salt

pepper

Pour the lentils onto a plate and pick through them for any pebbles or small clumps of soil, then place them in a sieve and rinse well. Finely dice the onion, celery, and carrot (about ¼ inch/6 mm). Strip the kale leaves from the stems, finely chop the stems, and cut the leaves into wide pieces.

Pour a good amount of olive oil (4 table-spoons/60 ml) into a medium, heavy-bottomed saucepan and add the garlic and sage. Heat over medium until the garlic is aromatic, but not browned, 2 to 3 minutes. Add the pancetta and render the fat, about 3 minutes. Stir in the chopped onions, carrots, celery, and kale stems and season with salt and pepper. Cook until the vegetables soften, about 10 minutes. Stir in the kale leaves, coating them with fat.

Add the lentils and enough water to cover them by about 1 inch/2.5 cm. Bring to a simmer. Stir the pot and reduce the heat to simmer gently. Cook partly covered until lentils are tender but retain their texture, about 40 minutes. Season with salt and pepper as needed.

Ceci in Zimino

CHICKPEAS AND SWISS CHARD

A stew of softly cooked Swiss chard (or other greens) with lots of olive oil is known as inzimino, a centuries-old term that evolved from Arabic. Various ingredients are cooked this way—most often chickpeas, cuttlefish, or calamari.

....

SERVES SIX

2 cups/360 grams cooked
   chickpeas in cooking liquid
   (page 227), or two 15 ounce/
   425 gram cans

3 bunches Swiss chard
   (1¼ pounds/570 grams)

3 large garlic cloves

salt

chili flakes

6 tablespoons/90 ml extra-virgin
   olive oil + more for serving

Drain the chickpeas into a bowl and reserve the liquid. Strip the Swiss chard leaves from their stems, and wash in a large bowl of cold water. Drain the leaves in a colander (leave some water clinging to the leaves). Tear the leaves into large pieces. Rinse the stems, and finely chop them. Coarsely chop the garlic cloves. Sprinkle a large pinch of salt and chili flakes onto the garlic and run your knife through them a few times, to make a coarse paste.

Add the garlic to a pot large enough to hold all the chard and pour the oil over it. Place over medium heat, stir, and cook until fragrant, but don't let the garlic brown (about 2 minutes). Add the chard stems and the leaves with water still clinging to them to the pot, stirring as they cook down. When all the greens have wilted, add the chickpeas and 1¼ cups/300 ml of their cooking liquid (or water). Cover the pot and cook until the greens are soft and dark, and the liquid has almost completely reduced, 25–30 minutes. Season with salt as needed and finish with a generous pour of olive oil.

Ceci

CHICKPEAS

Add a few leaves of herbs if you like, such as bay leaves, sage, or fresh thyme.

....

MAKES 2 CUPS/360 GRAMS
COOKED CHICKPEAS

1 cup/200 grams dried chickpeas
1 garlic clove
fresh herbs, optional
extra-virgin olive oil
salt

Pour the chickpeas onto a plate and pick through them for any pebbles or clumps of soil, then place them in a sieve and rinse well. Place them in a bowl, cover with about 3 inches/7 cm cold water, and soak overnight.

The next day, drain the chickpeas and place them in a pot with enough space for them to double in size. Cover with cold water by about 2 inches/5 cm and add the garlic, and the herbs if using. Bring to a boil and skim off any foam that rises to the top. Pour in a splash of olive oil (about 1 tablespoon/ 15 ml). Reduce the heat so beans are simmering gently, cover the pot, and cook until tender, 40 minutes to 1 hour, depending on freshness. Stir in 1 teaspoon/3 grams of salt and continue cooking gently for 10 minutes. If not using them right away, cool the chickpeas in their liquid, and then refrigerate for up to 5 days, or freeze for up to 3 months.

Fagioli all'Uccelletto

CANNELLINI WITH SAGE, TOMATO, AND SAUSAGE

Serve these beans piping hot with bread for dipping.

SERVES SIX

extra-virgin olive oil

3 sweet Italian sausages

2 garlic cloves, crushed

4 fresh sage leaves

one 28 ounce/794 gram can crushed tomatoes (3 cups)

4 cups cooked Cannellini (page 140)

salt

pepper

Preheat the oven to 375°F/190°C. Heat a large, ovenproof sauté pan over medium-high and coat generously with oil (about 2 tablespoons/30 ml). Slice the sausages open lengthwise and crumble the filling directly into the pan (discard the casings). Add the garlic and sage and cook until the sausage is browned, stirring occasionally. Add the tomatoes, stir, and reduce the heat to medium-low. Cook until the sauce is thick and glossy, 10 to 15 minutes.

Stir in the beans with a large pinch of salt, and season with pepper. Finish cooking in the oven until the edges are crusty and browned, 25 to 30 minutes. Drizzle the surface with olive oil just before serving.

THE FARMYARD

I grew up on a fattoria, or farm. I had to help with
the chores like other farm children. My family
were all contadini, or farm workers; they were from
Mugello, north of Florence. On our property, we
grew vegetables and fruits, and kept chickens,
ducks, and rabbits in the farmyard, which we call
an aia. We also raised pigs for meat and cows for
milking.

RITA

Coniglio Fritto

FRIED RABBIT

Frying bread with rabbit was one of the frugal ways that Rita's family used to make the most of the small farm's yield. We batter thick slices of country bread and serve them that way at Via Carota because they taste so good together. Both the rabbit and the fried bread are best picked up and eaten with your hands.

....

SERVES FOUR

4 rabbit hind legs
5 cups/1¼ liters Brine (page 350)
½ loaf day-old country bread
3 large eggs
4 large sprigs fresh rosemary
3 tablespoons/45 ml water
1 cup/140 grams cornstarch
1 cup/120 grams all-purpose flour
safflower oil for frying, about
    3 cups/720 ml
extra-virgin olive oil for frying,
    about 3 cups/720 ml
salt
8 cloves of garlic, unpeeled

Cut each rabbit leg into three pieces. You can do this with a cleaver or a strong knife, separating each leg from the thigh at the joint, and then cutting each thigh through the bone into two pieces. Place the rabbit in a container and cover with brine; cure for at least 8 hours and up to 2 days in the refrigerator.

Cut the bread into 4 thick slices (about 1 inch/2.5 cm), large enough to hold two pieces of rabbit.

Prepare your setup for frying the rabbit and the bread: Lightly beat the eggs in a medium bowl. Mince the leaves of 1 stalk of rosemary and add it to the eggs; add water to lighten the egg mixture and whisk to combine. In a separate bowl, sift the cornstarch and flour together. Set a paper towel–lined tray next to the stove.

Pour equal amounts of safflower and olive oil into a heavy, high-sided pot, to about 4 inches/10 cm deep, and heat over medium heat until a crumb of bread dropped in the oil sizzles immediately when it hits the oil (or a candy/deep-fry thermometer reaches 350°F/175°C). If the oil isn't ready, wait another minute or so.

Drain the rabbit and dip the still slightly wet pieces into the flour mixture, then the egg wash, and then back into the flour mixture, pressing to heavily coat the meat; shake off excess. Working in batches, gently drop the rabbit pieces into the hot oil. Fry until a metal skewer inserted into the thickest part of the meat feels hot to the touch once you pull it out, and the juices run clear (not at all pink), about 8 minutes, or until 160°F/71°C. Transfer to paper towels, and sprinkle lightly with salt. Repeat with the rest of the rabbit. Then fry the bread—dipping first into egg, then flour.

While the rabbit is frying, add the remaining stalks of rosemary to the pan to crisp along with the garlic cloves with their skin on. Serve pieces of rabbit on top of the fried bread, with fried rosemary and the caramelized garlic cloves.

Cibreo

CHOPPED CHICKEN LIVERS

This is a rich version of chopped liver on toast; eat it with a knife and fork, a cloth napkin in your lap, and a glass of Chianti.

....

SERVES FOUR

1 pound/454 grams fresh chicken
    livers
extra-virgin olive oil
1 medium red onion (8 ounces/
    225 grams), finely chopped
salt
10 fresh sage leaves, finely chopped
all-purpose flour for dredging,
    about ½ cup/60 grams
1½ cups/360 ml dry white wine
freshly grated nutmeg
pepper
½ cup + 2 tablespoons/150 ml
    chicken stock, divided
4 thick slices country bread
1 clove garlic, halved crosswise
2 large egg yolks
1 lemon
flaky sea salt

Rinse the chicken livers in a colander, handling them gently. Use a paring knife to trim away any stringy membranes, separating the two "lobes." Place on a kitchen towel and pat dry; cut each "lobe" in half. Coat the bottom of a medium saucepan with olive oil, set over medium heat and add onions with a large pinch of salt. Cook, stirring occasionally until the onions are golden and soft, about 8 minutes. Stir in the sage.

Meanwhile, place the flour in a shallow bowl and season it with ¾ teaspoon of salt. Dredge the livers, a few pieces at a time. Shake off excess flour as you transfer them to a plate. Set a large skillet over medium-high and coat the bottom with oil. When the oil is shimmering, add the livers in a single layer—don't crowd the skillet (cook them in two batches if necessary). Cook without turning until browned on the first side; then cook on the other side until lightly browned, 5 to 8 minutes total.

Spoon the livers into the pot of onions, raise the heat to medium-high, and stir in some wine (about ¼ cup/60 ml)—as it bubbles, it will make a sauce to lightly coat the livers. Season with a few gratings of nutmeg, salt (about ¼ teaspoon), and pepper. Add the rest of the wine, and ½ cup/120 ml chicken stock (set aside about 2 tablespoons/30 ml for later). Reduce the heat to medium and cook at a gentle simmer, stirring often, until

the sauce is thick and creamy and begins
to stick to the bottom of the pot, 45 to 50
minutes. Coarsely mash the livers with your
spoon.

Lightly brush the bread with oil and grill or
toast on both sides. While the bread is still
warm, rub it with the cut sides of the garlic.

To finish preparing the cibreo, heat the
remaining 2 tablespoons/30 ml of chicken
stock. Whisk egg yolks with 2 tablespoons
lemon juice in a small bowl until pale and
frothy; temper the egg yolks by slowly
pouring the hot stock into them and whisking
until warm. Stir into the chicken livers until
combined into a silky sauce, 1 to 2 minutes.
Season with salt and pepper and a squeeze
of lemon, if needed. Spoon hot cibreo over
the grilled bread, drizzle with olive oil and
sprinkle with sea salt.

Pici all'Anatra

HAND-ROLLED SPAGHETTI WITH DUCK RAGÙ

Once duck legs are cooked until tender, their pulled meat and braising liquid create a rich sauce for pasta. You can prepare the Pasta di Semola (page 365) and roll the pici while the duck legs are cooking.

SERVES FOUR

FOR THE DUCK RAGÙ

1 large carrot

1 celery stalk

1 medium onion

½ cup/120 ml duck fat or extra-
   virgin olive oil

1 bay leaf

salt

3 duck legs (2–2¼ pounds/
   900 grams–1 kg total)

½ cup/120 ml red wine, such as
   Chianti

1 cup/240 ml Vegetable Broth
   (page 348), or water

1 cup/250 grams canned crushed
   tomatoes, or puree (passata)

1 tablespoon/15 grams tomato
   paste

pepper

14 ounces/400 grams Pici
   (page 238)

Parmigiano Reggiano for serving

Finely dice the carrot, celery, and onion. Heat a large, heavy pot with a lid over medium heat and add the duck fat or olive oil and the bay leaf. When the oil is hot, add the carrots, celery, and onions and ½ teaspoon/1.5 grams salt and cook until soft, about 10 minutes. Push the vegetables to the sides and add the duck legs to the pan with the fat side down; cook for about 10 minutes so the vegetables continue to soften in the fat and absorb the flavor. When the bottom of the legs are golden, flip them and pour in the wine. Simmer until the alcohol has evaporated (about 2 minutes), then add the stock or water and cook uncovered until reduced by about half (10 to 15 minutes). Add the crushed tomatoes and tomato paste and season with salt and pepper. Turn the duck legs in the sauce once to coat them and return to skin side up. Reduce the heat to low and cover the pot. Cook over low heat until the duck is so tender that the meat can be pulled into pieces, 1½ to 2 hours.

Remove the duck from the heat and use two forks to pull the meat into strips and small pieces, discarding the bones and fat. Return the duck to the sauce to heat through, about 10 minutes. Taste for salt and pepper, adjusting as needed.

Bring a large pot of water to a boil and salt it generously (about 2 tablespoons/18 grams). Cook the pici in batches until they are al dente, 8 to 10 minutes (add the thickest ones to the pot first). Reserve about 1 cup/240 ml of pasta cooking water before draining. Add the pici to the sauce in the pan and add about half the cooking water, stirring to loosen the sauce. Add a little more water if needed to coat the pici. Serve with grated parmigiano.

Pici

HAND-ROLLED SPAGHETTI

Pici are the simplest form of hand-rolled pasta. Roll and stretch ropes of dough under your hands until they are like thick spaghetti with pointed ends.

SERVES FOUR

semolina flour for rolling
14 ounces/400 grams Pasta di Semola (page 365)

TO MAKE THE PICI Have ready a sheet pan dusted with semolina. Divide the dough in half. Cover half with a bowl while you work. With a rolling pin, roll the dough on a very lightly floured board until you have a sheet about ⅓ inch/5 mm thick. Cut the pasta sheet into short pieces (1–2 inches/2.5–5 cm). Roll a piece of pasta between your hands into a short rope, then place on the board. Place the palms of your hands on top of the pasta rope, and with fingers outstretched, roll the dough back and forth. Work gradually toward the ends to lengthen the dough. Continue rolling and stretching outward until the rope is thin (the pici will expand when cooked) and about 10 inches/25 cm long. Don't try to make them perfect; they will be irregular. Lay the pici out on the sheet pan with space between them, and sprinkle with semolina to prevent them from sticking. You can cook them immediately or let them dry until firm.

MAIALE/PORK AND CURED PORK PRODUCTS

Each fall, my family would butcher a pig. Then, every piece of the animal would be transformed into something edible; rigatina (bacon), or guanciale, similar to pancetta, seasoned with herbs and spices, made from the animal's jowl instead of belly. We'd store the meat from the pig and our homemade cheese in a room that faced north and remained dark and cooler throughout the year. We never took any ingredient for granted—it had been carefully raised and then slaughtered on the farm to feed our big family.   **RITA**

Braciole al Latte

PORK CHOPS COOKED IN MILK

Cooking pork in milk keeps the meat from drying and accentuates its mild sweetness. When the pan comes out of the oven, the chops are bathed in a highly seasoned, milky sauce. Special dishes often require planning ahead, and like most of our white and lean meats, we brine these pork chops for a day or two before cooking.

....

SERVES FOUR

2 bone-in pork chops, about 2 inches/5 cm thick
1 recipe (10 cups/2.5 liters) Brine (page 350)
extra-virgin olive oil
1 cup/240 grams Strutto (page 354)
4 large garlic cloves
8 leaves of lacinato kale, stems removed
Fennel Seed Salt (page 357)
1½ cups/360 ml whole milk

Brine the pork chops for 2 days. Before cooking, remove from the brine, pat them dry, and bring to room temperature. Preheat the oven to 400°/200°C.

Lightly coat a large, ovenproof skillet with olive oil (about 1 tablespoon/15 ml) and add 2 tablespoons/30 grams of strutto; heat over medium until the fat begins to render. Meanwhile, rub the pork all over with the rest of the strutto. Place the pork chops in the hot skillet with space between them. Crush the garlic cloves with the side of a knife and add to the pan. Raise the heat to medium-high and cook the chops on both sides until deeply browned, about 5 minutes per side (if the loose bits of strutto begin to burn, push them to the edges of the pan). Add the kale leaves, nestling them between the pork chops. Sprinkle everything with fennel seed salt, then pour in the milk. Once the milk is simmering, transfer the pan to the oven and cook until the pork is medium-well to well done (or 155°F/68°C to 160°F/71°C), about 12 to 16 minutes.

Transfer pork chops to a plate and tent with foil. Return the skillet to the stove over medium-high heat and stir the kale leaves. Bring to a simmer, and reduce the sauce for 5–8 minutes while the pork rests. Pour in any collected juices from the plate—there should still be enough sauce in the pan to spoon over the pork. Slice the pork and spoon the kale leaves and sauce on top.

TIP · STRUTTO

We often use cured pork to season pork. It's a great way to add fat and depth of flavor to cuts that are on the lean side. Strutto (page 354) is a robust paste made from cured pork and pork fat with garlic and herbs, ground together. It makes use of fatty scraps and pork trimmings, plus any pancetta and prosciutto ends. We season it with Fennel Seed Salt (page 357) and keep a jar in the walk-in refrigerator.

Rigatina con Cipolline

ROASTED PORK BELLY WITH LITTLE ONIONS

Crisp yet tender, our bacon dreams.

SERVES FOUR

4 thick slices (1 inch/2.5 cm)
   Rigatina (page 351)
extra-virgin olive oil
½ pound/225 grams cipollini
   onions, or substitute 6 small
   shallots
salt
pepper
2 sprigs fresh rosemary
6 tablespoons/90 ml balsamic
   vinegar

Preheat the oven to 450°F/230°C. Lightly coat a large skillet with oil and lay the pork slices in the center. Add onions or shallots with a large pinch of salt, pepper, and the rosemary. Roast without disturbing until the pork is sizzling and the onions are browned and tender, about 30 minutes.

Turn the onions and the pork and return to the oven to brown the second side, 8 to 10 minutes. Pour off most of the fat, keeping about 1 tablespoon/15 ml in the pan. Pour vinegar into the hot skillet and stir to coat the onions. Spoon the onions and sticky pan juices over the pork belly.

OLIVE OIL

....

In the hills north of Florence, farm families like the Sodis made wine from their grapes and, of course, pressed olive oil from their own olive trees. Our olive oil comes from the Mugello area, old trees grown by the Sodi family and family friends. The raccolta (harvest) begins in early November. Olives are raked from under the trees, sacks filled and delivered to the local frantoio, where the olives are cold-pressed under stone mills. These mills run twenty-four hours a day throughout November.

The quality of olive oil, like wine, depends on nature, the growing season, temperature, and the rain. But unlike wine, oil tastes best and is best to use in the first year when serving with bread and tomatoes and fresh vegetables. Our recipes accentuate the flavor of olive oil. Fettunta, a plain piece of grilled bread rubbed with garlic, can be transformed with a drizzle of extra-virgin olive oil and pinch of salt. Pinzimonio, a plate of raw, crisp vegetables, accompanied by a small bowl of extra-virgin olive oil seasoned with salt, highlights the flavor of first-pressed peppery olive oils.

JODY & RITA

Pinzimonio

CRUDITÉS AND FIRST-PRESSED OLIVE OIL

*Set out a colorful arrangement
of autumn produce and a
small bowl of the best olive oil
seasoned with salt and pepper.
There is nothing more to it. Cut
everything into small pieces that
can be picked up and eaten out
of hand.*

SERVES FOUR

½ cup/120 ml extra-virgin olive oil

salt

pepper

assorted seasonal vegetables for dipping,
    such as:

2 Belgian endives, quartered through the core

1 radicchio di Treviso, leaves separated

2 carrots with tops, quartered lengthwise

1 fennel bulb, cut into spears

6 radishes, whole or halved

¼ head cauliflower or broccoli Romanesco,
    in florets

Torta all'Olio

OLIVE OIL CAKE

We pour warm honey syrup over our cake when it comes out of the oven—it soaks into the cornmeal crumb, keeping it moist. We also add a dusting of fennel pollen and sea salt at the last moment for aroma and texture. If you can't find fennel pollen, try our simple Fennel Seed Salt (page 357) as a substitute for both.

....

MAKES ONE 9 INCH/23 CM CAKE, SERVES EIGHT

FOR THE SYRUP

¾ cup/255 grams wildflower honey

½ cup/120 ml warm water

FOR THE CAKE

1 cup/240 ml extra-virgin olive oil + more for pan

1½ cups/180 grams all-purpose flour + more for pan

¾ cup/120 grams medium-grind cornmeal

1½ teaspoons/6 grams baking powder

½ teaspoon/3 grams baking soda

1 teaspoon/3 grams salt

3 large eggs

1 cup/200 grams sugar

zest and juice of 1 orange (about 2 teaspoons zest, ¼ cup/60 ml juice)

¾ cup/180 ml whole milk

TO SERVE

2 teaspoons/2–3 grams fennel pollen

flaky sea salt

Combine honey and water in a small saucepan and bring to a boil. Reduce heat and simmer gently until the consistency of light maple syrup, about 5 minutes. Set aside to cool until ready to use or refrigerate for up to 1 week.

Preheat the oven to 350°/175°C. Brush a 9 inch/23 cm round cake pan with olive oil and dust it with flour. Turn the pan upside down to tap out excess flour. Whisk the flour, cornmeal, baking powder, baking soda, and salt in a medium bowl. In a larger bowl, or the bowl of a mixer, combine the eggs, sugar, and the orange zest. Beat until egg mixture is pale and creamy, about 3 minutes. Pour in the olive oil, milk, and orange juice, stirring to blend. Add the flour mixture into the liquid ingredients in two batches, stirring until combined in a smooth batter.

Pour into the prepared pan and jiggle to settle the surface. Bake, rotating once, until golden brown on top and a skewer inserted in the center comes out clean, 40 to 45 minutes. Let cool for 30 minutes on a wire rack. Remove the cake from the pan, place on a rimmed plate, and drizzle honey syrup evenly over the surface; let it soak in for at least 15 minutes. Just before serving, sprinkle the cake with fennel pollen and sea salt.

Panna Cotta all'Olio

OLIVE OIL PANNA COTTA

Extra-virgin olive oil makes each spoonful of panna cotta lighter on the palate than when it's made with only cream and milk. A little olive oil on top along with sea salt accentuates the savory/sweet contrast. Serve with a dollop of bright fruit preserves—Marmellata di Kumquat (page 272) in winter, and Conserva di Rabarbaro (page 74) in spring.

....

MAKES 4 SERVINGS

1 cup/240 ml whole milk

1 cup/240 ml heavy cream

ice water

1½ teaspoons/5 grams unflavored, powdered gelatin

¼ cup + 1 heaped tablespoon/ 70 grams sugar

⅓ cup/80 ml olive oil

flaky sea salt

Combine milk and cream in a small saucepan. Heat over medium until there are a few small bubbles around the edges of the pot, but don't let the cream mixture boil. Remove from the heat.

Pour 2 tablespoons/30 ml ice water into a medium bowl and sprinkle the gelatin over it. Let stand until it softens and blooms, about 2 minutes. Whisk the hot cream into the gelatin. Prepare a large bowl of ice water and set the bowl of cream in it to cool. Whisk occasionally until cold to the touch. Pour the cold cream mixture into a blender jar (or use an immersion blender).

Combine the sugar and olive oil in a medium bowl and whisk them vigorously for about 30 seconds; then with the blender running, pour the olive oil into the cream in a slow, steady stream to emulsify. Divide panna cotta among four 4 ounce/120 ml cups and place them on a tray. Refrigerate until set, at least 4 hours—panna cotta should wiggle slightly when you shake it. Serve with a drizzle of olive oil and a tiny pinch of flaky sea salt.

FRUIT AND NUTS

A slice of raw apple. A handful of walnuts with a wedge of cheese. A pear hot out of the oven. Almonds and jam fill our favorite tarts. This is autumn.

Pere al Vino Rosso

BOSC PEARS ROASTED IN RED WINE

These pears are sugared and almost blackened in the oven— brutti ma buoni (ugly but beautiful). We display them on the marble table in the dining room during the season.

SERVES SIX

6 ripe Bosc pears
2 cups/480 ml red wine
½ cup/100 grams sugar
1 cinnamon stick

Preheat the oven to 400°F/200°C. Nestle the pears together in an ovenproof skillet, standing up against each other. Pour the wine over the pears and sprinkle the tops with sugar. Add the cinnamon stick to the pan.

Roast until the pears are caramelized on top and completely tender when pierced with a fork, about 45 minutes. Let the roasted pears rest in the wine until you serve them.

Crostata di Lamponi

RASPBERRY JAM TART

A slice of this crostata can be breakfast, dessert, or a teatime treat.

You will need a 9 inch/23 cm pastry tin with a removable bottom.

....

MAKES ONE 9 INCH/23 CM
TART, SERVES EIGHT

1 recipe Pasta Frolla (page 369)
all-purpose flour for rolling
half a lemon
1–1¼ cups/300–375 grams seedless
    raspberry jam
1 egg, beaten with a splash of water

Follow the recipe for pasta frolla and divide the dough into two disks of different sizes (about two thirds and one third). Chill for 1 hour before rolling.

Bring the large disk of dough out of the refrigerator and let it soften slightly, about 10 minutes; it should be malleable but still feel cool to the touch. Dust a wooden board with flour and have extra flour on the side. Roll the dough into a circle about 10 inches/25 cm in diameter, using flour to dust the board and the rolling pin as needed. Lift the dough by loosely wrapping it around the rolling pin and carefully transfer to a 9 inch/23 cm pastry tin with a removable bottom. Don't worry if the dough breaks, just patch any cracks or tears. Press the dough firmly into the bottom of the tin and trim the edges. Fold any overhanging dough against the sides, making the sides thicker than the bottom. Flatten the rim so it's flush with the top of the tin. Refrigerate or freeze the tart shell until firm, at least 1 hour, up to overnight.

Roll out the smaller disk of dough and cut into strips about ½ inch/2 cm wide (we use a fluted-edged wheel, but a knife or a pizza wheel works just as well) and transfer to a piece of parchment or a baking pan; refrigerate or freeze until firm, about 1 hour.

Preheat the oven to 375°F/190°C with a rack in the center. Remove the tart shell from the refrigerator and prick the bottom in several places with a fork.

Squeeze lemon juice into the jam to taste (about 2 teaspoons/10 ml) and spread it evenly onto the chilled tart shell. Take the strips of dough from the refrigerator and cut or weave them to make a lattice top. (At this point, the crostata can be baked immediately or chilled overnight before baking.)

Brush the pastry lattice and the edges with the egg wash and bake the crostata until the edges and top are deep golden brown, about 35 minutes, rotating the pan once. Set on a wire rack to cool.

Crostata di Mandorle

ALMOND TART

This golden-brown tart is nutty and not too sweet, and it's simple to make.

You will need a 9 inch/23 cm pastry tin with a removable bottom.

....

MAKES ONE 9 INCH/23 CM TART, SERVES EIGHT

1 disk (half recipe) Pasta Frolla
    (page 369)
all-purpose flour for rolling
Almond Filling, chilled (page 260)
1½ cups/160 grams sliced,
    blanched almonds
confectioners' sugar for dusting

Take the dough out of the refrigerator and let it soften slightly, about 10 minutes; it should be malleable but still feel cool to the touch. Dust a wooden board with flour and have extra flour on the side. Roll the dough into a circle about 10 inches/25 cm in diameter, using flour to dust the board and the rolling pin as needed. Lift the dough by loosely wrapping it around the rolling pin and carefully transfer to a 9 inch/23 cm pastry tin with a removable bottom. Don't worry if it breaks, just patch any cracks or tears. Press the dough firmly into the bottom of the tin and trim the edges. Fold any overhanging dough against the sides, making the sides thicker than the bottom. Flatten the rim so it's flush with the top of the tin. Refrigerate or freeze the tart shell until firm, at least 1 hour, up to overnight.

Preheat the oven to 375°F/190°C. Prick the pastry bottom in several places with a fork. Fill the tart shell with almond filling and spread evenly. Scatter the sliced almonds on top, covering the filling completely. Bake until the almonds and crust are golden brown, and the filling has puffed slightly, 30 to 35 minutes. Set on a wire rack to cool. Dust with confectioners' sugar before serving.

ALMOND FILLING

8 tablespoons/115 grams unsalted
    butter, room temperature

½ cup/100 grams sugar

2 large eggs

1 tablespoon/15 ml almond liqueur

2½ cups/300 grams almond flour
    (or finely ground almonds)

½ teaspoon/1.5 grams salt

Cream the butter and sugar together until fluffy and pale in a bowl, or in an electric mixer with the paddle attachment. Add the eggs 1 at a time, blending thoroughly after each addition. Stir in the almond liqueur, almond flour, and salt, and mix to a smooth paste. Refrigerate for at least 30 minutes before using. The filling can be refrigerated for up to 1 week.

Cantuccini
TWICE-BAKED ALMOND COOKIES

We serve these little biscotti with desserts, such as roasted pears or panna cotta, and they make sweet parting gifts, wrapped up and tied with a ribbon.

....

MAKES ABOUT 3 DOZEN

¾ cup/100 grams almonds

3 tablespoons/45 grams unsalted
    butter, softened

¾ cup/150 grams sugar +
    1 tablespoon/10 grams for
    sprinkling

2 large eggs, 1 separated

2 cups/240 grams all-purpose
    flour

1 teaspoon/4 grams baking
    powder

salt

3 tablespoons/45 ml cold water

Preheat the oven to 375°F/190°C. Spread the almonds on a sheet pan and toast until fragrant, 5 to 6 minutes. Slide onto a plate to cool completely.

Reduce the oven temperature to 300°F/150°C. In a large bowl, work the butter and sugar together with a wooden spoon until creamed. Beat in 1 egg and 1 egg yolk (reserve the white). In a separate bowl, whisk together the flour, baking powder, and add about ¼ teaspoon/1 gram salt. Stir this mixture into the butter mixture. Add 2 to 3 tablespoons/ 30 to 45 ml water, as needed to make a soft, compact dough. Add the almonds, mixing them in with your hands.

Line a sheet pan with parchment. Divide the dough in half on the pan and firmly shape into two logs, each about 1¾ inches/4 cm wide, and 1 inch/2.5 cm high.

Lightly beat the remaining egg white and brush it over the logs, then sprinkle them generously with sugar. Bake, rotating the pan once, until the logs are lightly golden and firm when pressed, about 50 minutes. Slide the parchment onto a wire rack and cool the logs completely, about 30 minutes.

Reduce the oven temperature to 250°F/120°C. Have ready a parchment-lined pan. Use a serrated knife to thinly slice the logs (¼ inch/6 mm) and lay them flat on the pan. Bake until firm and dry in the center, about 10 minutes. Set on a wire rack to cool completely before storing. Cantuccini will keep for 3 weeks in an airtight container.

6

Winter

The feasting season begins! Bring on the
truffles, roast the chestnuts . . . pour out
the magnums. Boxes of panettone tied with
ribbons fill our shelves and the sideboard
glows with sugar-dusted cakes. Via Carota's
kitchen reaches its crescendo in December.
The festive mood transcends our own hustle
to ensure that our guests' spirits are lifted
during their time with us.

CITRUS

....

Lemons, mandarins, and deep blood oranges
arrive at our door just when we need to burst out
of darkness. We fill large earthenware crocks and
decorate the dining room with them.

Insalata di Arance

ORANGES, RED ONIONS, AND OLIVES

A cheerful arrangement of bright oranges; any varieties will do.

SERVES FOUR

4 blood oranges

2 small, sweet oranges such
    as mandarin or cara cara,
    or tangerines

quarter of 1 red onion

⅓ cup/60 grams olives, such
    as arbequina, nocellara,
    or castelvetrano

1 garlic clove

1 tablespoon/15 ml aged sherry
    vinegar

salt

pepper

3 sprigs fresh oregano

¼ cup/60 ml extra-virgin olive oil

6 fresh basil leaves

Peel the oranges neatly by slicing off the tops and bottoms, so the oranges sit flat on a cutting board. Use a paring knife to slice off the peel from top to bottom, following the orange's curve (make sure to shave off all the white pith). Collect any juices from the cutting board into a small bowl. Slice each orange into 5 or 6 rounds and arrange them on a plate.

Finely slice the onion and soak the slices in a bowl of cold water for a minute or two. Drain in a fine-mesh sieve and pat them dry with a kitchen towel. Rinse the olives and pat them dry. Pit them and lightly crush into large pieces.

Scatter the onions and olives over the orange slices. Finely grate the garlic into the bowl of collected orange juice, and add the vinegar, a pinch of salt, and pepper. Finely chop the oregano leaves and stir them in. Slowly whisk in the olive oil. Spoon the dressing over the salad and sprinkle with basil leaves.

Risotto al Limone

MEYER LEMON RISOTTO

Meyer lemons with a few basil leaves perfume the rice. Vibrant extra-virgin olive oil, instead of butter, adds the finishing touch to this lemon risotto.

SERVES FOUR

2 Meyer lemons

piece of Parmigiano Reggiano,
    4 ounces/115 grams

6 cups/1.5 liters water

extra-virgin olive oil

5 fresh basil leaves

1 large shallot, finely chopped

1½ cups/300 grams risotto rice,
    such as nano vialone

½ cup/120 ml dry white wine

salt

pepper

Zest the lemons and juice them into a cup. Finely grate the parmigiano; you will have about 2 handfuls. Bring the water to a simmer in a medium pot. Coat a wide, heavy saucepan with oil (about 2 tablespoons) and warm 3 basil leaves in it over medium heat until fragrant, about 1 minute. Remove the basil leaves and discard them. Add the shallots to the pan, cook them until soft, 2 to 3 minutes, then add the rice. Using a wooden spoon, stir constantly until the grains of rice are glossy and well coated, about 2 minutes. Raise the heat to high and pour in the wine, stirring until evaporated.

Add 2 teaspoons/6 grams salt to the pot of water. One ladleful at a time, add hot water to the rice, and stir until it's completely absorbed. Continue adding hot water gradually, only adding more when the rice is ready to absorb it; you will know it's ready when the bubbling increases and the spoon leaves a slow trail in the rice. Stir after each addition of water and cook until the rice is loose and creamy, and when you bite into a grain of rice it's barely tender, 18 to 20 minutes (you might have about ½ cup/120 ml of water left).

To finish, stir in the lemon zest and juice. Pour in a stream of olive oil (about 2 tablespoons/30 ml), stirring the risotto vigorously at the same time. Stir in the parmigiano; add salt if needed. Tear 2 basil leaves in half and stir them into the risotto. Grind pepper over each serving, and drizzle with olive oil.

Marmellata di Kumquat

KUMQUAT MARMALADE

We spoon this light marmellata onto creamy desserts such as Panna Cotta all'Olio (page 251) and Torta di Ricotta (page 76).

....

MAKES TWO 10 OUNCE/
284 GRAM JARS

1 pound/454 grams kumquats
   (3 cups)
1 lemon
1¾ cups/420 ml water
2½ cups/500 grams sugar

Place the kumquats in a bowl of water, scrub them well, and rinse them. Pick off any hard stems. Slice the kumquats into very thin rounds with a sharp or serrated knife. As you slice, flick out the seeds with the tip of your knife and reserve them. Put the kumquats into a container big enough to hold them, with some extra space.

Peel the lemon and very finely slice the peel; juice the lemon. Pour the lemon juice through a strainer (you should have about ¼ cup/ 60 ml juice) into the container of kumquats; save any seeds. Wrap the reserved kumquat seeds with the lemon seeds in a piece of cheesecloth, tie it tightly with twine, and place the bundle in the container. Add the lemon zest and pour in the water. Cover and set aside overnight.

The next day, have ready two sterilized jars with lids (see instructions for sterilizing jars, page 352). Put the sugar in a wide pot and pour the kumquats, the cheesecloth bundle, and their soaking liquid over the sugar. Make sure the bundle is submerged. Heat the pot very slowly over medium-low to dissolve the sugar, about 5 minutes. When it begins to bubble, raise the heat to medium-high and bring to a boil. It will bubble and foam actively. Cook without stirring for 10 minutes or until the marmellata looks glossy or reads 220°F/105°C on a candy/deep-fry thermometer. Stir the marmellata gently.

Turn off the heat and let stand for 10 minutes. If it looks runny, don't worry—it will thicken a little as it cools. Press the cheesecloth bundle with tongs to squeeze any syrup it has absorbed into the pot, then discard the bundle. Ladle the hot marmellata into jars, leaving ⅛ inch/3 mm of space. Cover jars tightly and cool to room temperature. Refrigerate for up to 2 months.

NOTE When cooking marmellata, getting to just the right setting point is not a perfect science; there are many factors involved. Some kumquats have more seeds than others, and because the seeds contain pectin (a natural setting agent), each batch of marmellata is different. Soaking the seeds in water helps to bring out the pectin and soften the kumquat slices, producing a delicate mixture. We add the juice and zest of a lemon too, as well as their seeds for pectin. We keep our marmellata in the refrigerator. To make shelf-stable marmellata, follow safe canning instructions.

RADICCHIO

Winter brings forth just what you need at the right time, like bitter radicchio and other chicories that cut through the rich foods of the season.

Radicchio Trevisano

GRILLED RADICCHIO WITH GOAT CHEESE, CURRANTS, AND PINE NUTS

Radicchio Trevisano is elegant with smooth, elongated leaves. Any radicchio can be substituted here; if you use a larger variety, cut it into quarters and be sure to keep a bit of the core attached to each wedge.

SERVES FOUR

2 tablespoons/15 grams dried currants

¼ cup/60 ml warm water

¼ cup/60 ml aged sherry vinegar or red wine vinegar

2 heads radicchio Trevisano, halved lengthwise through the core

extra-virgin olive oil

salt

¼ cup/60 ml Via Carota Vinaigrette (page 340)

2 tablespoons/20 grams pine nuts, toasted

2 ounces/55 grams soft goat cheese

Place the currants in a cup and soak them in warm water and vinegar until soft and plump, about 30 minutes; drain though a fine-mesh sieve.

Preheat a grill or a heavy grill pan over medium-high heat. Brush the radicchio with olive oil and salt and grill, turning occasionally, until lightly browned and wilted, about 10 minutes. Toss it in a bowl with vinaigrette and transfer to a plate. Sprinkle with pine nuts and the currants and crumble goat cheese on top.

Insalata con Castelfranco

WHITE RADICCHIO, ROBIOLA, AND
TOASTED HAZELNUTS

*Speckled Castelfranco is less
bitter than other chicories. We
combine it with other radicchio
for a mix of textures. Make
substitutions if you like but
keep them in the chicory family.
The honey and hazelnuts are a
match for the wintery leaves.*

SERVES TWO

1 head radicchio Castelfranco
    (12–16 leaves)
8 leaves radicchio di Treviso
salt
3 tablespoons/45 ml Robiola
    Vinaigrette (page 341)
3 tablespoons/40 grams
    hazelnuts, toasted and skinned
    (see note below)
1 small spoonful fresh thyme
    leaves and tender tops
flavorful wildflower honey

Combine the Castelfranco and other
radicchio leaves in a large bowl, season with
salt, and toss with dressing, mixing with your
hands to coat the leaves thoroughly. Coarsely
chop the hazelnuts. Sprinkle the salad with
hazelnuts and thyme leaves and drizzle with
honey.

TIP · REMOVING THE SKINS FROM
HAZELNUTS

To toast and skin hazelnuts, spread them
onto a pan and toast at 350°F/180°C until
they smell nutty, 5 to 8 minutes. While
they're still warm, rub them briskly with a
kitchen towel to remove their papery skins.

FENNEL

A palate cleanser when raw, fennel complements
the more robust flavors at the table—and when it's
roasted or grilled, it mellows to a deep sweetness.
Fennel should be firm and full in the hand when
you buy it. Save any trimmed stalks and use them
in stocks; save the fresh inner fronds for adding to
Salsa Verde (page 346) and sprinkling into salads.

Insalata di Finocchio

SHAVED RAW FENNEL WITH OLIVES

A mandoline comes in handy for achieving feathery slices of fennel. We prefer a Tuscan pecorino, aged sixty days, for this salad.

SERVES FOUR

2 fennel bulbs

piece of pecorino cheese, about
   3 ounces/85 grams

12 pitted olives, such as nocellara
   or castelvetrano, chopped into
   large pieces

2 tablespoons/30 ml Colatura
   Dressing (recipe below), or
   to taste

extra-virgin olive oil

COLATURA DRESSING

4 teaspoons/20 ml colatura
   (see note)

4 teaspoons/20 ml water

1 small garlic clove

pinch chili flakes

Trim the fennel, cutting off the outer layer if browned or scuffed. Reserve the prettiest fronds and chop them. Halve the fennel bulbs lengthwise and cut out their cores. Thinly shave on a mandoline or slice very thinly with a sharp knife. Place in a salad bowl.

Break up the pecorino into small rough pebbles with the tip of a paring knife. Add the olives. Toss the salad with the dressing, adding a little olive oil to taste.

FOR THE COLATURA DRESSING Stir colatura and water together in a small bowl. Finely grate the garlic directly into the bowl and add the chili flakes.

TIP · COLATURA

When anchovies are salted, stacked, and pressed for a long period of time (sometimes up to three years), they give off a pungent, clear liquid. The ancient Romans used a similar method to make their famous seasoning garum; while garum was made with fish innards, colatura makes use of the whole fish. Colatura is a unique, artisanal condiment made on the Amalfi coast of Italy. It's sold in little bottles—a very small amount adds deep notes to a dish.

Finocchi alla Cenere

CHARRED FENNEL WITH ORANGE AND HONEY

2 large fennel bulbs

salt

2 bay leaves, dried or fresh

1 large orange

3 tablespoons/65 grams
   wildflower honey

extra-virgin olive oil

juice from about half a lemon

chili flakes, optional

Bring a medium pot of salted water to a boil. Trim away the outer layer of the fennel bulbs if they're brown or scuffed. Cook whole fennel bulbs in boiling water until the tip of a knife can be easily inserted into the center (20 to 25 minutes). Drain in a colander and let them air dry for 10 minutes.

Preheat a grill or grill pan to high and char the fennel thoroughly on all sides (or hold it over the flames on the stovetop, turning it with tongs as it blackens). Briefly grill the bay leaves. Peel a large strip of orange rind with a vegetable peeler and grill it for a minute or two to release its aromatic oils.

Squeeze the juice of the orange (about ¼ cup/60 ml) into a medium saucepan and add the honey, grilled bay leaves and orange peel, olive oil (about 1 tablespoon), and a squeeze of lemon; add a pinch of salt, and chili flakes if desired. Place over high and bring to a boil, then reduce heat to low. Cut the fennel into wedges through the core, add them to the pan, and stir to coat them in the syrupy juice.

CARDOONS

The cardoon stands alone. A cousin of the artichoke, it is beloved for its subtle flavor, which is like celery and artichoke combined.

Eat the small, inner ribs raw, dipped into Bagna Cauda (page 309). Most often we slice cardoon ribs into bite-sized pieces, poach them until tender, and then fry them until crisp.

Cardi Fritti

FRIED CARDOONS AND SAGE

We serve these crisped cardoons with a few fried sage leaves tucked in for a savory note. And there is one more surprise: as you pull one cardoon after another from the stack, you'll discover whole cloves of mellow garlic, bursting out of their skins.

SERVES FOUR

3 quarts/2.8 liters strained Court Bouillon (page 349)
6 cardoon ribs (about 1 pound/ 454 grams)
1¼ cups/150 grams all-purpose flour
1¼ cups/175 grams cornstarch
salt
extra-virgin olive oil for frying, about 3 cups/720 ml
safflower oil for frying, about 3 cups/720 ml
8 garlic cloves, skin on
8 fresh sage leaves
piece of Parmigiano Reggiano, about 3 ounces/85 grams, for serving

Bring court bouillon to a boil in a medium pot. Using a vegetable peeler or paring knife, pull off the tough outer strings from the cardoon ribs. Slice the ribs into 3 inch/ 8 cm lengths. Gently drop the slices in the court bouillon and simmer until very tender, about 30 minutes. Let them cool in the liquid. Before frying, drain the cardoons in a colander.

Sift the flour, cornstarch, and a pinch of salt in a large bowl. Pour equal amounts of olive and safflower oil into a deep, heavy pot until 2 to 3 inches/5 to 7 cm deep. Heat the oil over high heat, about 8 minutes. Test the oil to see if it's ready; if you drop a breadcrumb or a small piece of cardoon into the pot it should sizzle and float the moment it hits the oil. A candy/deep-fry thermometer clipped on the side of the pot should read 350°F/175°C. While the oil is heating up, line a sheet pan with a few layers of paper towel and set it next to the stove.

Drop a handful of blanched cardoons into the flour mixture and toss to coat thoroughly. Shake off excess flour. Fry the cardoons in batches, turning occasionally, until golden and crisp, 3 to 4 minutes. Transfer from the oil onto the paper towels and sprinkle with salt. Repeat with the rest of the cardoons, adjusting the heat as needed between batches to maintain the temperature. Test the oil for temperature before adding each new batch.

Fry the garlic cloves until lightly browned, about 5 minutes, and lift them out. Add the sage leaves to the oil and fry just until crisp (about 30 seconds), then drain on the paper towels. Gently toss the cardoons, garlic, and sage together and finely grate parmigiano over the top.

TIP · CHOOSING CARDOONS

When you buy cardoons, avoid any with spongy ribs. Trim off the tops and the shaggy leaves and pull off the strings that run along each rib. We don't bother putting them in acidulated water; we work quickly, paring knives in hand, and as soon as we have a nice pile trimmed and sliced, we drop them into a pot of court bouillon to cook them until tender.

ROOT VEGETABLES

Choose an assortment of roots based on what looks firm. Create a colorful mix and make substitutions.

Salsify and scorzonera are interchangeable. Both are long, slender roots—salsify is light brown while scorzonera is black on the outside. They both become creamy when cooked. Just like potatoes, they turn brown once peeled. We don't worry about keeping the roots perfectly white since we like to brown them in the pan anyway. Most salsify roots are thin; peel them and then cut into pieces of the same length. Any spears thicker than your thumb should be cut in half lengthwise.

Scorzonera al Burro

SALSIFY IN BROWN BUTTER AND GARLIC

For a vegetable that looks like the root of a small tree, salsify is surprisingly delicate when cooked. We baste it in browned butter; it absorbs the caramelized flavor and takes on a burnished look.

SERVES FOUR

4 scorzonera or salsify roots, peeled

extra-virgin olive oil

2 garlic cloves

salt

3 tablespoons/45 grams unsalted butter

4 stems fresh thyme

Cut the salsify into 6 inch/15 cm lengths. Coat the bottom of a large skillet with oil (about 1 tablespoon/15 ml) and place over medium-high heat. Lay the salsify in the pan in a single layer. Press down on the garlic cloves with the flat side of a knife to split open the skin; add the garlic in its skin to the pan.

Turn the salsify in the oil and sprinkle with salt; add the butter to the pan. After it melts and foams, add the thyme. Spoon the butter over the salsify from time to time as it browns; it will coat it with brown flecks. Cover the pan to reduce spattering, reduce the heat to medium, and cook until browned on all sides, lifting the lid and turning the salsify and basting with butter occasionally, 5 to 7 minutes. A knife cutting through the salsify should meet little or no resistance.

Arrange the salsify and garlic cloves on a warmed plate and spoon the browned butter from the bottom of the pan over them.

Tuberi al Forno

ROASTED TURNIPS, CELERY ROOT, AND PARSNIPS

To peel celery root, use a sharp knife to slice off the gnarled ends before peeling off the outer layer.

. . . .

SERVES FOUR

2 medium turnips (12 ounces/
   340 grams)
2 parsnips (12 ounces/340 grams)
1 salsify root (4 ounces/115 grams)
½ celery root (8 ounces/
   225 grams)
salt
extra-virgin olive oil
4 large garlic cloves
6 sprigs fresh thyme
3 tablespoons/45 ml Via Carota
   Vinaigrette (page 340)

Preheat the oven to 450°F/230°C. Peel all the vegetables. Cut them into various shapes: cubes, wedges, and spears, in similar sizes. Season the vegetables generously with salt and coat with olive oil, tossing with your hands. Spread in a single layer on a sheet pan with the garlic cloves and thyme sprigs.

Roast the vegetables without stirring until browned on the bottom, and tender—the thickest pieces should be easily pierced with the tip of a knife, about 30 minutes. Toss with the vinaigrette while warm.

POTATOES

Choose starchy baking potatoes like russets for making topini and gnocchi dough, and waxier boiling varieties—such as our house favorite, the flavorful Yukon golds—for most everything else.

Patate all'Ortolana

CRUSHED POTATOES AND CARAMELIZED
SHALLOTS

*While they're in the pan, crush
these potatoes and fold with
caramelized shallots.*

SERVES FOUR

1¼ pounds/570 grams small
    potatoes, such as Yukon gold
salt
extra-virgin olive oil
1 shallot, finely chopped
2 garlic cloves, finely chopped
1 tablespoon fresh thyme leaves,
    from about 4 sprigs, finely
    chopped
4 fresh sage leaves, finely chopped

Peel and halve the potatoes, place them in a
medium pot, and cover with cold water. Add
1 teaspoon of salt and bring to a boil. Cook
until the potatoes are completely tender,
about 18 minutes, then drain them.

Meanwhile, pour a generous amount (about
5 tablespoons/75 ml) of olive oil into a large
skillet, add the shallot, garlic, thyme, and
sage and set over medium-low heat. Sprinkle
lightly with salt. Cook the garlic and shallots
until very soft, but not browned, about 5
minutes. Raise the heat to medium and add
the potatoes. Break them up with a spatula,
and stir to coat with the shallot mixture.
Leave the potatoes alone to brown on the
bottom, 5–10 minutes, and then stir in the
browned bits. Cook, pressing down from
time to time, and folding in the herbs and
shallots, about 15 minutes.

Patate Fritte

FRIED POTATOES, GARLIC, AND SAGE

Via Carota fried potatoes are cut by hand, just like at home. We add sage and garlic cloves. Note that we are shallow-frying here—instead of submerging the potatoes in a deep pot of oil, the potatoes and oil should be pretty much at the same level.

....

SERVES FOUR

1¾ pounds/800 grams medium
    yellow potatoes, such as
    Yukon gold
4 large garlic cloves, skin on
safflower oil for frying, about
    1½ cups/360ml
extra-virgin olive oil for frying,
    about 1½ cups/360ml
flaky sea salt
8 fresh sage leaves

Peel the potatoes and cut them into pieces the size of your finger. Soak them in cold water for 2 hours, up to overnight. Drain and spread the potatoes out onto a clean kitchen towel; pat them dry. Press on each unpeeled garlic clove with the heel of your hand just to break the skin; do not peel.

Pour both oils into a wide, straight-sided pan to come up about 1½ inches/4 cm. Place over high heat—the oil is ready when a sage leaf sizzles the moment it hits the oil. If it doesn't, heat the oil a little bit longer. Meanwhile, line a sheet pan with paper towels and set it next to the stove. Carefully add the potatoes, garlic, and sage leaves to the hot oil and stir gently to spread them into an even layer. The oil should be at the same level as the potatoes; they do not all need to be covered by oil. Adjust heat to medium-high and cook until potatoes are golden brown, 30 to 35 minutes, turning them only one or two times while they're cooking. Adjust the heat as needed to keep the oil bubbling actively.

Lift the garlic and potatoes out of the oil with a spider or slotted spoon and spread them out on the paper towels. Sprinkle with salt and add the sage leaves.

NOTE If you would like to save the frying oil so it can be used for future frying, cool it to room temperature, strain it into a bottle, and store for up to 1 month.

FRIED POTATOES

In my family, fried potatoes were usually eaten at a
weekend meal. My mother always cut them by hand—
and she soaked them in cold water for at least two
hours. **RITA**

Topini Mugellana

POTATO GNOCCHI

Very small and round, topini are named after field mice.

....

SERVES FOUR

2½ pounds/1.1 kg starchy potatoes, such as russet (Idaho)

¾ cup/90 grams all-purpose flour, or as needed

1 large egg, lightly beaten

salt

about half a nutmeg, finely grated (about 1 teaspoon)

2 cups/1 batch Sugo Povero (page 304) or Sugo di Carne (page 303)

piece of Parmigiano Reggiano, about 3 ounces/85 grams, finely grated, for serving

Preheat the oven to 425°F/220°C. Prick a few holes in the unpeeled potatoes and bake them until tender when pierced with a fork, about 45 minutes. When cool enough to handle, cut off their skins with a paring knife.

Lightly flour a large, flat surface and put the peeled potatoes through a potato ricer or food mill onto the surface. Make a well in the middle and add the egg, 2½ teaspoons/7.5 grams salt, and the nutmeg. Sprinkle ½ cup/60 grams of flour over the mixture, and gently mix to form a soft dough. Handle the dough as little as possible, gathering it together. Use a bench scraper or spatula to lift the potatoes and fold the dough onto itself; sprinkle just as much flour as needed to hold it together. The dough should not stick to your fingers. Pack it into a thick slab and divide in three.

Flour your hands and roll each portion of dough into a long rope approximately ¾ inch/2 cm in diameter. Keep the remaining dough covered with a kitchen towel while you work. Lightly flour your workspace as needed and cut the ropes into 1 inch/2.5 cm pieces. Gently roll the pieces into balls about the size of a marble between your hands (a shape referred to as topini—little mice). Transfer topini to a floured sheet pan and shake the pan a few times to coat them with flour. Cover the pan with a kitchen towel while you roll the remaining dough.

Let the topini rest for 20 minutes before cooking. Bring a large pot of generously salted water to a boil. Add the topini, lower the heat to medium, and cook until they float to the surface, about 2 minutes—do not let the water boil while they're cooking.

Meanwhile, warm the sauce in a large pan and transfer the topini with a spider or slotted spoon directly into the sauce, tossing to coat. Serve with a dusting of parmigiano.

....

TIP · GNOCCHI RULES

The key to making light gnocchi and topini is to use only as much flour as you need to hold the dough together, and to work quickly while the potatoes are hot. So add flour incrementally, beginning with less than the recipe says, and know that you will be adding quite a bit more to coat the work surface and your hands as you go.

While the gnocchi sit and wait to be cooked, give them a little extra dusting of flour, and roll them in it; they sometimes soften and stick to the pan. To safeguard against that, it helps to cut three strips of parchment to fit your sheet pan and place the rolled gnocchi on the parchment—when it comes time to drop them in the water, you simply pick up a parchment strip and roll the gnocchi into the water. Never let gnocchi or topini boil in the water—just simmer gently so they don't disintegrate.

HOME COOKING

A good meal at home is proof of time well spent.
If you put most everything aside to spend the day
chopping vegetables, simmering a ragù for hours,
or rolling out pasta sheets, you know this to be
true.

THE MEZZALUNA

I understood many things about Rita's mother, Elena, just by standing in her modest kitchen. I remember that her kitchen was small, efficient, and pristine even though it had been used daily for most of her lifetime. Waiting on the oven door there were twin crochet potholders that I am sure she made, worn out from years of feeding the family. On a low wooden table rested a cutting board with a brass handle and a mezzaluna on it. The board was no bigger than a book and it was stained green from chopping herbs, with quite an impressive, deep groove down the middle from constant use. The image is forever embedded in my mind. I never met her; we only spoke on the phone a few times talking briefly about the weather before she would remind me to take good care of Rita in New York City. When she died, the family gathered around the table, connected by their loss and sorrow, to share a meal in Elena's honor. The meal was traditional Florentine dishes that Rita and I spent days preparing at her home in Bagno a Ripoli.

JODY

Jody joined me in Italy the day after my mother's funeral. It was June, almost ten years ago. My family gathered for lunch the next day to honor my mother, so there wasn't much time for anything but cooking. We put on our aprons and got started. We kneaded pasta, rolled out topini, chopped celery, carrots, and onions to braise beef shanks that the local butcher dropped off with condolences. Aunts and uncles stopped by throughout the day to help clean artichokes and shell peas. I learned to cook from my mother, and to this day I still compare my dishes to hers. I inherited her respect for food and her passion for cooking. Her handwritten recipes and notes are some of my dearest possessions.

After days of preparation, the family finally sat down together; there must have been thirty people gathered around two long tables. We squeezed into my mother's tiny kitchen to add the finishing touches. Bottles of wine were brought up from the cellar, and we poured and toasted to my mother's life, and to all she had given us.

When Jody and I left for New York, we brought Mamma's mezzaluna and cutting board back. They hold pride of place at Via Carota in the old oak hutch next to the vintage dessert plates, decanters, and bowls of lemons.

RITA

Lasagna Cacio e Pepe

WHITE LASAGNA

We've stopped at ten layers. But once you get rolling, you may want to keep going—add as many pasta sheets as you can confidently pile into the baking pan and watch the sauce bubble over the sides.

SERVES EIGHT

salt

Besciamella al Pecorino (page 300)

32 strips of pasta, each approximately 4 x 9 inches/ 10 x 23 cm (page 302)

8 ounces/225 grams finely grated pecorino Romano + more for serving

Bring a large pot of salted water to a boil. Meanwhile, lightly coat the bottom of an ovenproof dish (9 x 13 inches/23 x 33 cm) with pecorino bechamel sauce. Set the dish near the stove. Have ready a double layer of kitchen towels, or a clean tablecloth like Rita's mother used to do.

Reduce the heat so the water is just shy of boiling. Gently lower three sheets of pasta into the water. Stir the pasta gently to keep them from sticking, cook until they float, about 1 minute. Lift the pasta out with a spider and lay it flat on the kitchen towels to dry—if the pasta is folded or stuck together, dip it in water again.

Place pasta in the baking dish (use about two and a half sheets, trimming the sheets to fit as necessary, and saving the trimmings). Spread a thin layer of pecorino bechamel sauce over the pasta and sprinkle with pecorino cheese. Cook three more sheets of pasta. Repeat with another layer of pasta, lightly covering it with sauce and pecorino. When all the pasta is layered in the dish, spread the top with a bit of sauce and sprinkle with pecorino.

Let stand about 30 minutes, or up to 2 hours, to set before baking. Preheat the oven to 400°F/200°C. Bake the lasagna uncovered until golden and bubbling hot, 30 to 40 minutes. Sprinkle the surface with grated pecorino just before serving.

BESCIAMELLA AL PECORINO

PECORINO BECHAMEL SAUCE

An abundant amount of black pepper, combined with pecorino Romano stock, gives a simple bechamel sauce the flavors of cacio e pepe.

. . . .

MAKES ABOUT 2 QUARTS/
2 LITERS

1 quart/1 liter whole milk
8 tablespoons/113 grams unsalted butter
1 cup/120 grams all-purpose flour
1 quart/1 liter Pecorino Stock (page 301)
salt
coarsely ground pepper (about 2 tablespoons/20 grams)
about half a whole nutmeg

Heat the milk in a saucepan over medium heat until steaming, then remove from the heat. Melt the butter in a medium, heavy-bottomed saucepan over low heat, and whisk in the flour in a few additions. Switch to a wooden spoon when it becomes too thick for the whisk and stir the smooth paste over low heat for 2 minutes. Gradually pour in the hot milk, whisking until thoroughly combined and there are no lumps.

Heat the pecorino stock in the empty saucepan and whisk it into the sauce. Season with salt (about 1 teaspoon/3 grams), and the pepper, and finely grate nutmeg into the pot. Cook over low heat, stirring the bottom occasionally until you have a creamy sauce the consistency of thin pancake batter, about 15 minutes. Let cool for at least 30 minutes while you cook the pasta sheets. The sauce can be refrigerated up to 3 days.

PECORINO STOCK

Collect your pecorino Romano rinds and scraps. When you have enough, use them to make a pot of stock. This can be made with parmigiano rinds too.

....

MAKES ABOUT 6 CUPS/
1.5 LITERS

½ pound/225 grams pecorino Romano rinds and scraps
about 3 quarts/3 liters water

Scrub cheese rinds with a stiff brush, peel off any labels, and rinse them. Place the rinds and scraps of pecorino in a medium pot. Cover with cold water by 2 to 3 inches/5 to 7.5 cm and bring to a boil. Lower the heat and simmer very gently for 30 minutes. Let stand for 15 minutes, then skim fat and impurities from the top. Strain the stock before using. The stock can be refrigerated for several days.

LASAGNA SHEETS

MAKES 32 SHEETS OF PASTA,
CUT FOR LASAGNA

semolina, or all-purpose flour
28 ounces/800 grams Pasta di
Semola (page 365)

Have ready a sheet pan lightly dusted with
semolina or flour. Have a few clean kitchen
towels on hand. It's useful to have a rolling
pasta cutter, but a sharp knife will do. Divide
the dough into 8 wedges. Work with one
portion at a time, keeping the remaining
portions covered with a bowl to prevent them
from drying out as you work.

Flatten one portion of dough with the heel of
your hand until it's about ½ inch/1.5 cm thick.
Feed it once through the widest setting (#1)
of the pasta machine. Fold the dough into
thirds and rotate it 90 degrees to pass the
narrow side of the rectangle through setting
#1 again. Repeat a couple of times until
the dough is smooth and even. Adjust the
machine to the next setting (#2) and pass the
dough through it twice. Feed through each
subsequent setting one time until it's thin
enough to see the shadow of your hand. Cut
the dough into 4 lengths. Lay them flat on the
pan, and cover with a kitchen towel. Repeat,
keeping the rolled pasta sheets covered while
you work.

If not cooking it right away, cover the pasta
with a kitchen towel and wrap tightly with
plastic wrap. Pasta can be refrigerated for
up to 24 hours.

Sugo di Carne

FOUR-HOUR MEAT SAUCE

A soffritto of onions, celery, and carrot cooked in a generous amount of olive oil until completely soft and golden adds profound flavor to a sauce. In Rita's kitchen, you are not allowed to remove the lid of this meat sauce except to stir once in a while—she is strict about cooking it covered for about four hours, so it becomes dark, and rich.

SERVES EIGHT

⅓ cup/80 ml extra-virgin olive oil

9 medium red onions (2¼ pounds/1 kg), finely diced

6 celery ribs, finely diced

3 large carrots (14 ounces/ 400 grams), finely diced

3 pounds/1.4 kg ground beef, 80% lean

salt

pepper

3 cups/720 ml dry white wine

3 cups/750 grams canned crushed tomatoes, or puree (passata)

1 cup/240 ml water

Heat the oil in a large, wide pot with a heavy bottom (8 quarts/7.4 liters) over medium heat; add the onions, celery, and carrots, and a large pinch of salt. As the vegetables cook slowly, they will perfume the kitchen. Cook, stirring often with a wooden spoon, until very soft and golden, 30 to 40 minutes. When they begin to stick to the pot, this is the moment to add the meat. Raise the heat to medium-high and stir in the beef, breaking it up with a fork. Season with 1 teaspoon/3 grams salt and a little pepper and cook, stirring occasionally, until the meat has released its water and begins to brown and stick to the bottom of the pan, 10 to 15 minutes.

Add the wine, and season with salt and pepper again. Reduce the heat to medium-low, cover the pot, and cook at a very low simmer until the meat starts to stick to the bottom, about 45 minutes. Spoon off any excess fat. Season with salt and pepper; stir the tomatoes and water into the sauce. Cover the pot and cook at a bare simmer, stirring every once and a while, for about 3½ hours. The sauce is done when it is thick and the liquid is well reduced; if there is a little pool of fat on the top, spoon it off. Taste for salt and pepper.

The sauce can be cooled, transferred to a container, covered, and refrigerated for 3 to 5 days, or frozen for 1 month.

Sugo Povero

SLOW-COOKED VEGETABLE RAGÙ

Some weeks, Rita's family had more vegetables in storage than meat, so Rita learned to make this sauce. Serve just as you'd serve the Sugo di Carne (page 303).

SERVES EIGHT

⅓ cup/80 ml extra-virgin olive oil

9 medium red onions
　(2¼ pounds/1 kg), finely diced

2 bunches celery, finely diced

9 carrots (12 ounces/340 grams),
　finely diced

salt

pepper

3 cups/720 ml dry white wine

2½ cups/625 grams canned
　crushed tomatoes, or puree
　(passata)

1 cup/240 ml water

Heat the oil in a large, wide pot with a heavy bottom (8 quarts/7.4 liters) over medium heat; add onions, celery, and carrots, a large pinch of salt, and pepper. As the vegetables cook slowly, they will perfume the kitchen. Cook, stirring often with a wooden spoon, until the vegetables are very soft and golden, 30 to 40 minutes. When they begin to stick to the pot, raise the heat to medium-high and pour in the wine; let it simmer until evaporated.

Stir the tomatoes and water into the sauce, and season with salt (about 1½ teaspoons/ 5 grams), and a little pepper. Reduce the heat to medium-low, cover the pot, and cook at a bare simmer, stirring every once in a while, for about 3½ hours. Add up to 1 cup water during the cooking time if the sauce is sticking to the pot. The sauce is done when the liquid is reduced so the sauce is thick but not dry. Season with salt and pepper as needed.

If not using right away, cool the sauce to room temperature, then transfer to a covered container and refrigerate for about 5 days, or frozen for 1 month.

Svizzerina

HAND-CHOPPED STEAK

Svizzerina is seasoned only on the outside, just like a good steak. We sear to a deep brown, with a rare midsection. The meat must be chopped by hand, and all the trimmed fat is added back to the meat for flavor and moisture.

MAKES 1 SVIZZERINA, SERVES TWO

8 ounces/225 grams New York strip steak

1–2 ounces/28–56 grams fat, optional (see tip box)

salt

1 tablespoon/15 ml oil from Garlic Confit (page 355)

3 cloves from Garlic Confit (page 355)

1 large stem fresh rosemary

flaky sea salt, for sprinkling

Make sure your knife is very sharp, and the steak is cold. Trim off the fat cap and remove any small bits of hard gristle; set the fat aside in the refrigerator (discard any gristle). Thinly slice the steak across the grain about ¼ inch/6 mm. Cut the slices into thin strips and freeze them until firm, about 5 minutes. Resharpen the knife and dice the strips into the smallest possible cubes. Run your knife through the meat once or twice until finely chopped.

Very finely chop the chilled, reserved fat. Using a light touch, mix to evenly distribute the lean and the fat. Form into a thick patty (about 1½ inches/4 cm thick). Refrigerate until ready to cook.

Season both sides generously with salt. Heat a small, heavy skillet over medium-high. When the pan begins to smoke, pour in a little garlic confit oil and sear a deep brown crust on the bottom of the patty, 2 to 3 minutes. Gently flip the svizzerina and add the garlic cloves to the pan. Cook the second side for 1 minute for rare (the patty should be just slightly springy around the edges when pressed, and soft in the middle). Add the rosemary sprig to the pan to sizzle.

Serve the svizzerina with the rosemary and the garlic cloves, still in their skins. Drizzle lightly with garlic oil and sprinkle with flaky sea salt.

TIP · MORE FAT

FAT EQUALS FLAVOR: Buy well-marbled, untrimmed steaks so you can use the cap fat. We like our svizzerina to be 20 percent fat. If your steaks don't have a large fat cap on them, ask a butcher to give you an extra 1 to 2 ounces/30 to 55 grams of trimmed fat for each svizzerina you're making.

CHOPPING TIPS: For slicing and chopping the steak, have a metal bowl set inside a larger bowl of ice and place the meat into the smaller bowl to keep it cold.

SALT, CAPERS, AND ANCHOVIES

Salt and time work wonders together. When highly perishable anchovies and cod are left to cure in salt for days, their textures become firmer and their flavors deepen—this is what makes us want to keep dipping into a bowl of bagna cauda, and it's what differentiates baccalà from more neutral fresh cod. Salt preserves fresh, green caper buds so we can eat them all year long. It also works as thermal protection; when coarse salt is piled around a whole branzino it creates a rock-solid chamber that keeps moisture inside, a simple and time-worn method for baking delicate fish.

Bagna Cauda

RADISHES, ANCHOVY, GARLIC, AND OLIVE OIL

This anchovy bath from Piemonte is addictive. Bagna cauda should be enjoyed warm. It makes sense to serve it in the cold months with the crunchy peppery vegetables of the season. We choose radishes.

SERVES FOUR

FOR THE BAGNA CAUDA

4 large garlic cloves, crushed

extra-virgin olive oil

6 meaty anchovy fillets
+ 1 teaspoon/5 ml of their oil

3 tablespoons/45 grams unsalted
butter

salt

**RADISHES AND OTHER
VEGETABLES FOR DIPPING**

6 radishes

½ fennel bulb

1–2 Belgian endives

¼ head cauliflower or broccoli
Romanesco

2 hearts of little gem or romaine
lettuce

1 carrot

half a lemon

4 Uova Barzotte

Place the garlic in a very small, heavy pot and pour in enough olive oil to cover it (about ½ cup/120 ml). Cook over the lowest possible heat until the garlic is soft, about 10 minutes. Use a fork to smash the garlic in the pot. Turn off the heat and add the anchovies plus a teaspoon of their oil to the pot. Mash the anchovies with a fork and return the pot to low heat; cook until the anchovies have dissolved into a paste, about 5 minutes. Off the heat, stir in the butter and season with salt if needed. Keep bagna cauda warm while you prepare the crudités.

Wash and trim all the vegetables. Cut them into pieces that can be easily dipped into the bagna cauda; keep the radishes whole. Cut long spears of fennel and endive, florets of cauliflower, and wedges or tiny hearts of lettuce with some of their tops still attached. Cut the carrot into long pieces and squeeze lemon over them. Arrange everything in a pretty way. Peel the eggs, cut them in half, and add to the plate.

UOVA BARZOTTE

Place 4 large eggs in a small pot and cover with cold water by about 1 inch/2.5 cm. Bring to a boil and immediately turn off the heat. Set a timer for 5 minutes.

Prepare a small bowl of ice water, and as soon as the timer goes off, scoop out the eggs and drop them into the water. Let sit for a few minutes; when the water becomes warm, refresh with cold water. Crack the shells and return eggs to the water for a minute before peeling.

Crostini Tonno, Caperi e Burro

TUNA AND CAPER BUTTER ON TOAST

Spread this piquant butter generously onto thick slices of toast.

....

MAKES ENOUGH FOR 12 TOASTS

8 tablespoons/113 grams unsalted
    butter, at room temperature
1 cup (4 ounces/115 grams) Tonno
    Sott'Olio (page 356)
3 tablespoons/45 grams salt-
    packed capers, rinsed and
    chopped + more for serving
1 tablespoon/15 ml lemon juice
4 large sprigs fresh flat-leaf parsley
salt
pepper
12 thick slices of country bread

Cream the butter in a large bowl with a wooden spoon. Lift the tuna out of the oil and stir it into the butter, breaking it up with a fork. Stir in the capers and lemon juice. Finely chop the parsley and stir it in. Season with salt (about ¼ teaspoon/1 gram) and pepper. This can also be made in a food processor—pulse the machine so the tuna doesn't get completely creamed. Some flakes of tuna should still be visible in the butter.

Toast the bread on both sides and spread a large spoonful of tuna butter on it while the toast is still warm. The tuna butter should be almost as thick as the bread slices. Refrigerate any remaining tuna butter for up to 1 week.

....

TIP · CAPERS

After caper buds are picked, they're either preserved in salt or pickled in brine. We recommend buying salt-packed capers whenever possible because the salting intensifies their vegetal flavor. Before using, they need to be soaked in warm water for about 5 minutes to rid them of excess salt, lifted out of the water to leave the salt behind, and rinsed.

Baccalà Mantecato

SALT COD WHIPPED WITH POTATOES AND
OLIVE OIL

*We start with fresh cod to make
our own baccalà, but if you have
a good source for salt cod fillet,
skip our salting instructions.
Buy a center-cut piece (avoid
the small wooden boxes of salt
cod; they tend to be filled with
end pieces). Serve baccalà with
grilled polenta (page 50) or
spooned onto toasted country
bread.*

....

MAKES ABOUT 2 CUPS

1 pound/454 grams fresh, skinless
   cod fillet (or salt cod)
2 cups/275 grams kosher salt
   + more as needed
½ pound/225 grams Yukon gold
   potatoes
1 cup/240 ml heavy cream
1 cup/240 ml whole milk, or as
   needed
2 garlic cloves
extra-virgin olive oil

Trim the cod, discarding any thin or fibrous pieces. Place the fish in a straight-sided dish that will fit in the refrigerator. Bury the cod in salt, about ½ inch/1.3 cm thick. Refrigerate until the fish is quite firm, about 7 days. It should be constantly covered by salt; check every 1 to 2 days to pour off any accumulated water and sprinkle with more salt as needed.

Thoroughly rinse the cod and soak it in a large bowl of cold water. Refrigerate for 2 to 3 days, replacing the water 3 times daily (or leave the bowl under a running tap for a few hours each day). To test if the fish is ready to eat, cut a small piece from the center and simmer it in water until tender, then taste for saltiness. If it's too salty, soak it in fresh water for another day.

Peel the potatoes, dice them into large cubes, and put them in a medium saucepan with the cream. Pour in enough milk to cover them and cook over medium-low heat until the potatoes are soft, about 20 minutes. Lift the potatoes out of the pot with a slotted spoon to make space for the fish and set them aside in a bowl.

Remove any pin bones from the cod and cut the fish into 2-inch pieces. Place in the pot of cream and add the garlic; cover and cook until it softens into tender flakes, about 10 minutes. Pour off and reserve about one third of the cream. Return the potatoes to the pot with the fish. Cook uncovered over low heat, stirring occasionally until most of the cream has reduced (20 to 30 minutes). Gradually pour olive oil into the pot while whipping with the spoon to make a dense puree, leaving some flakes of cod for texture. Add some reserved cream if needed to mellow the flavor. Serve warm or at room temperature over grilled polenta or toast. Baccalà keeps, refrigerated, for about 1 week.

Branzino al Sale

SALT-BAKED SEA BASS

This dramatic method ensures that your cooked fish will be moist and tender. Once cooked, there will be nothing to distract from the fish's flavor.

....

SERVES TWO

1 whole branzino (1–1½
   pounds/454–680 grams),
   gutted and scaled
3 lemon slices
4 stems fresh thyme
1 large egg white
5 cups/700 grams salt
extra-virgin olive oil for serving
flaky sea salt for sprinkling,
   optional

Preheat the oven to 400°F/200°C. Rinse the fish inside and out and pat dry. Place the lemon and thyme inside the cavity. In a large bowl, whisk the egg white until frothy. Pour the salt into the egg white in a steady stream, mixing with your hands until the mixture is the consistency of barely wet sand.

Pour about a third of the salt onto the center of a sheet pan, creating a bed a little bit larger than the fish. Place the fish on top and cover it with the rest of the salt mixture, packing it to encase the body of the fish, leaving the dorsal fin exposed (it's fine to leave the head exposed too). Bake until the dorsal fin can be easily wiggled and pulled off, 18 to 25 minutes, depending on the size of the fish.

Firmly tap the salt crust with the end of a kitchen spoon or the back of a large knife until it cracks open. Push the salt crust aside and brush any loose salt off the fish, and discard. To fillet the fish, make one long slice along the center from head to tail, then loosen the flesh on either side of the slice. Lift the cooked meat off the bones; flip the fish and repeat with the other side. Serve with a drizzle of olive oil and a sprinkle of salt if desired.

TRUFFLES

We have any number of vendors who we count on to bring us certain specialty items. Our truffle connection is one of those vendors. He shows up with two wicker baskets, lifts a cloth from the top of a basket, and Rita begins inspecting the contents. The scent of damp soil and pheromones rises above the table. There are black ones in one basket and white ones in another. Rita sorts through them, sniffing and touching them, checking the firmness of each truffle. She eventually selects several black ones and several white ones, keeping them in two separate piles. The black ones are strong, while the white ones are delicately perfumed. Each are used for distinct dishes. It is a seasonal ritual.

JODY *&* **RITA**

Bruschetta con Tartufo Nero

SHAVED BLACK TRUFFLES AND RICOTTA
ON TOAST

SERVES FOUR

1 black truffle

1 cup/250 grams whole-milk ricotta

salt

4 thick slices of country bread

flavorful wildflower honey

piece of Parmigiano Reggiano,
   about 2 ounces/55 grams

Thinly slice one half of the truffle, then finely dice the slices (reserve the other half of the truffle). Stir the diced truffles into the ricotta and season with salt. Toast or grill the bread and let cool slightly before spreading with the truffled ricotta. Drizzle each toast with honey. Use a vegetable peeler to shave parmigiano onto the toasts and shave the remaining truffle over the top.

Tagliatelle al Tartufo

FRESH PASTA WITH WHITE TRUFFLES
AND BUTTER

*What to do with your finest
treasure?*

....

SERVES FOUR

1 white truffle

½ cup + 2 tablespoons/140 grams
  cold unsalted butter

1 garlic clove

salt

12 ounces/340 grams fresh
  tagliatelle (page 324)

Thinly slice one half of the truffle, then finely dice the slices (reserve the other half of the truffle). Put 4 tablespoons/55 grams of butter in a large sauté pan—cut the remaining butter into small cubes and refrigerate them. Add the garlic to the pan of butter and melt over the lowest possible heat until the garlic is aromatic but not browned, about 5 minutes. Remove the garlic from the butter and discard it. Add the diced truffle and infuse the butter over very low heat until aromatic, about 10 minutes, and season with salt. Keep warm.

Bring a large pot of salted water to a boil. Separate the tagliatelle with your fingers into a loose pile and cook in the boiling water until al dente, 2 to 3 minutes. Stir while cooking to prevent the tagliatelle from sticking together. Reserve about 1 cup of the cooking water, then drain the pasta immediately to ensure it stays all dente.

Gradually add pieces of chilled butter to the warm truffle butter over medium heat, swirling the pan steadily, to allow the butter to emulsify with each new addition of butter. Toss the drained pasta into the pan and add about ½ cup/120 ml reserved cooking water. Add more pasta water as needed to coat the pasta in a creamy sauce. Serve in shallow bowls and finely grate the remaining truffle on top.

TAGLIATELLE

SERVES FOUR

all-purpose flour or semolina
12 ounces/340 grams Pasta Sfoglia
(page 363)

Have ready a sheet pan lightly dusted with flour or semolina. Have a few clean kitchen towels on hand. It's useful to have a pasta roller but a sharp knife will do. Divide the pasta dough into 4 portions. Work with one portion at a time and keep the remaining portions covered with a bowl to prevent them from drying out.

Flatten one portion of dough with the heel of your hand until it's about ½ inch/1.5 cm thick. Feed it once through the widest setting (#1) of the pasta roller. Fold the dough into thirds and rotate it 90 degrees to pass the narrow side of the rectangle through setting #1 again. Repeat a couple of times until the dough is smooth and even. Adjust the roller to the next setting (#2) and pass the dough through it twice. Feed through each subsequent setting one time until it's thin enough to see the shadow of your hand. Cut the dough into 3 or 4 lengths. Lay them flat on the pan, and cover with a kitchen towel. Repeat, keeping the rolled pasta sheets covered while you work.

Switch to the tagliatelle attachment or cut by hand. To cut by hand, take one sheet at a time, fold loosely into thirds (rolling onto itself) and cut into thin strips. Spread tagliatelle on the sheet pan; sprinkle lightly with flour or semolina and cover with a kitchen towel. Repeat with remaining pasta, dusting flour or semolina between the layers. If not cooking the pasta right away, cover it with a kitchen towel and wrap the pan tightly with plastic wrap. Pasta can be refrigerated for up to 24 hours.

CHOCOLATE AND NUTS

We reach for nuts and chocolate in the winter months, both for celebrations and quiet nights at home.

Torta al Cioccolato

FLOURLESS CHOCOLATE CAKE

After your cake rises beautifully in the oven, it will fall. Don't be disappointed, it is meant to do that. The top then forms a thin, crackly crust that contrasts with the light interior.

....

MAKES ONE 9 INCH/23 CM CAKE

1½ sticks/170 grams unsalted
    butter + more for the pan
cocoa powder or flour for the pan
7 ounces/200 grams bittersweet
    chocolate (1¼ cups chopped or
    morsels)
6 large eggs, at room temperature,
    separated
1 cup/200 grams sugar
¼ teaspoon salt

Preheat the oven to 350°F/175°C. Butter a 9 inch/23 cm springform pan. Dust the pan with cocoa or flour, and tip it upside down to tap out the excess.

Combine the chocolate and butter in a glass or metal bowl set over a pan of simmering water and stir occasionally until melted and thoroughly blended. Remove the bowl from the heat and let the chocolate cool slightly, about 15 minutes.

Whisk the egg yolks with ½ cup/100 grams sugar until pale and thick. In a separate bowl, whisk the egg whites, gradually adding the remaining ½ cup/100 grams sugar and the salt while you whisk, until the whites form stiff peaks. Stir the melted chocolate into the egg yolks. Gently fold the whipped egg whites into the chocolate mixture, allowing some streaks of egg white to remain. Pour into the prepared pan and shimmy the pan gently to settle the batter. Bake until puffed and the surface has formed a crust, 40 to 45 minutes. Don't bake this cake until it's completely firm, or it will be dry. Let cool completely on a wire rack before removing from the pan.

If you are not ready to bake right away, you can make the batter and refrigerate overnight before baking. We like to do this sometimes for the sake of convenience, and it gives the top crust more texture.

Tartufi al Cioccolato

CHOCOLATE TRUFFLES WITH GRAPPA

**8 ounces/225 grams bittersweet
    chocolate, chopped or morsels**
½ cup/120 ml heavy cream
2 tablespoons/30 ml grappa
salt
high-quality cocoa powder

Put the chocolate in a large mixing bowl. Stir together the cream, grappa, and a pinch of salt in a small saucepan over medium-high heat. When the cream is steaming, but before it comes to a full boil, pour it over the chocolate and let stand for 2 minutes to melt the chocolate. Vigorously whisk the chocolate and cream together until blended and completely smooth. Transfer the bowl to the refrigerator to cool until firm, stirring occasionally, about 1 hour. (At this point, the chocolate mixture can sit in the refrigerator, covered, for up to 1 week.)

Pour a pile of cocoa onto a plate. Drag a teaspoon across the surface of the solid chocolate repeatedly until you have a loosely piled spoonful. (If the chocolate is too hard to scrape, let stand at room temperature for a few minutes). Lightly press the chocolate with your hands to make a walnut-sized nugget and roll it in the cocoa powder. Avoid making the truffles perfect; they should be irregular and varied. Repeat with the rest of the chocolate. Transfer the finished truffles to a plate. Truffles keep well in the refrigerator for about 1 week but are best enjoyed at room temperature.

Semifreddo alla Gianduia

CHOCOLATE HAZELNUT SEMIFREDDO

The creamy blend of hazelnuts and chocolate known as gianduia is a signature of Piemonte. You will need an electric mixer for whipping the egg whites for this recipe.

....

SERVES EIGHT

4½ ounces (about 1 cup)/
    180 grams semisweet chocolate,
    chopped or morsels
½ cup/100 grams gianduia or
    other high-quality chocolate-
    hazelnut spread such as
    nocciolata
1½ cups/360 ml heavy cream
1 cup/200 grams sugar, divided
⅓ cup/80 ml water
4 large egg whites, at room
    temperature
salt
½ cup/60 grams hazelnuts,
    toasted and skinned (page 277),
    coarsely chopped
whipped cream for serving
unsweetened cocoa powder for
    serving
Croccante di Nocciole for serving
    (page 332)

Place an empty loaf pan in the freezer. Place the chocolate and gianduia in a metal or glass bowl set over a pot of simmering water; stir until mostly melted. Pour in the cream and stir to blend thoroughly. Remove from the heat and let cool to room temperature, stirring occasionally until semi-firm.

Set 2 tablespoons/25 grams of sugar aside and place the remaining sugar (¾ cup plus 2 tablespoons/175 grams) in a small saucepan. Pour the water over the sugar in the saucepan, and cook over medium heat until the sugar has completely dissolved. Raise the heat and bring to a boil; do not stir after it comes to a boil. When the syrup is the consistency of corn syrup, and a candy/deep-fry thermometer reads 238°F/114°C, remove the pot from the heat.

Place the egg whites and a large pinch of salt in the bowl of a mixer fitted with the whisk attachment. With the machine running on low speed, gradually add the reserved 2 tablespoons/25 grams sugar. Whisk to dissolve the sugar, about 2 minutes, then increase to high speed and whip until the whites form soft peaks.

With the machine still running, slowly drizzle the hot sugar syrup down the side of the bowl into the whipped egg whites until they form glossy, stiff peaks, 5 to 7 minutes. Use a spatula to gently fold in the melted chocolate and the chopped hazelnuts.

Fill the chilled loaf pan with semifreddo mixture, cover with plastic wrap, and freeze until firm, at least 4 hours, up to overnight. Semifreddo can be stored in the freezer for up to 2 weeks. Soften semifreddo in the refrigerator for at least 15 minutes or until it's fluffy enough to spoon. Serve in small glasses, dust with cocoa powder, and place a dollop of whipped cream on top. Sprinkle with croccante di nocciole.

Croccante di Nocciole

You will have extra! Sprinkle on affogato or other ice creams, or just eat as a treat.

....

MAKES 2½ CUPS

neutral oil, such as safflower, for pan
1 cup/200 grams sugar
⅓ cup/80 ml water
1 cup/140 grams hazelnuts, toasted and skinned (see note on page 277)

Line a small sheet pan with a silpat or parchment, or lightly coat it with oil. Place the sugar in a medium saucepan and pour water over it. Warm the pan over medium-high heat, stirring occasionally, until the sugar dissolves, 3 to 4 minutes. After sugar dissolves do not stir (swirl the pan gently, if necessary, for even browning). Reduce the heat to medium and cook until amber, 10 to 15 minutes. Immediately remove the pan from the heat.

Add the hazelnuts to the caramel, stirring carefully until coated. Pour them onto the prepared pan and, working quickly, spread the hazelnuts into a single layer with a spatula. Set aside to harden for about 15 minutes. Break the croccante into small pieces and coarsely chop them. The candied nuts can be stored in an airtight container at room temperature for up to 1 month.

Bruciate

ROASTED CHESTNUTS

We have a long-handled, perforated roasting pan, perfect for open flames, and a heavy cloth sack to keep the roasted chestnuts warm. Once the sack is full of hot charred chestnuts, we give it a couple of squeezes to help the skins break free.

....

SERVES TWO

2 pounds/1 kg fresh chestnuts
   of similar size
salt

Check the chestnuts and discard any that have stains or holes. Make a cut in the flat side of the chestnuts with a sharp paring knife, or a serrated knife, about 1 inch/2.5 cm. Make sure you cut only through the soft shell, and not the nut inside. This allows steam to escape, which is important for making sure the chestnuts won't burst during cooking. Transfer the chestnuts to a large bowl and cover with water. Leave to soak for 2 hours.

Heat a chestnut pan or a heavy cast-iron skillet over an open fire or on the stove over medium heat. Drain the chestnuts and place them in the pan. Reduce the heat to low (if using a stove), and slowly dry-roast until the skins are toasted and the meat is tender, shaking the pan from time to time, about 25 minutes.

Remove the chestnuts from the pan and wrap them in a kitchen towel. Leave for 15 minutes; this will make them easier to peel. Before serving, sprinkle the peeled chestnuts with salt.

You can find chestnuts roasting on nearly every corner in Florence in the winter, or so it seems. Hot off the coals, they are wrapped up in brown paper—nice for keeping your hands warm on a stroll through Piazza della Signoria. Our winter chestnut ritual at home in New York channels these moments on snowy nights when we light a fire in the fireplace. **JODY & RITA**

7

Basics

Essentials, odds and ends.

Here are the basics of what we keep stocked—as well as the finishing touches. We prepare many of these recipes in batches as part of our weekly routine and keep them in our refrigerator to use as needed.

VINAIGRETTES AND CONDIMENTS

These are part of our kitchen toolbox: the dressings the Via Carota team has committed to memory. They include all the vinaigrettes, which can be adapted to suit many seasonal dishes; the Salmoriglio we spoon over most things when they come off the grill (page 343); and a homemade mayonnaise (page 345) to use as a dip for grilled artichokes or fritti.

Via Carota Vinaigrette

It's a favorite. Enough said.

....

MAKES ABOUT 1 CUP/240 ML,
ENOUGH FOR 8 SALADS

1 shallot, very finely chopped
   (¼ cup)
1 garlic clove, finely grated
   (about ½ teaspoon)
¾ teaspoon/2 grams sugar
½ teaspoon/1.5 grams salt
6 stems fresh thyme
¼ cup/60 ml aged sherry vinegar
2 teaspoons/10 ml warm water
¾ cup/180 ml extra-virgin olive oil

Place the shallots in a fine-mesh strainer and rinse with cold water. Drain them and transfer to a small bowl with the garlic, sugar, and salt. Strip the thyme leaves off the stems and finely chop the leaves (for about 1 teaspoon thyme); stir into the bowl. Stir in the vinegar and water. Pour the olive oil into the bowl in a slow stream, whisking all the while until emulsified.

The vinaigrette can be refrigerated for up to 3 days.

Robiola Vinaigrette

MAKES ABOUT 1 CUP/240 ML,
ENOUGH FOR 4 SALADS

**one 100-gram package fresh
Robiolina cheese (about
7 tablespoons)**
**1 tablespoon/15 grams crème
fraîche**
salt
**½ cup/120 ml Via Carota
Vinaigrette (page 340)**

Whisk the Robiolina and crème fraîche together in a small bowl and add a couple of pinches of salt. Slowly pour in the vinaigrette, whisking constantly, until combined into a smooth dressing.

ROBIOLINA

Robiolina is a cow's milk cream cheese from Italy. With a soft and fluffy texture, it blends with other ingredients into a smooth dressing. This is nothing fancy—it's a common packaged cheese in Italian supermarkets. It's harder to find here, so if you can't locate Robiolina, double the crème fraîche in the dressing and use whipped cream cheese in its place; thin it with a splash of water while whisking. And what to do with the extra crème fraîche? Serve it with Pere al Vino Rosso (page 254) or Torta al Cioccolato (page 327).

JODY & RITA

Dried Porcini Vinaigrette

We suggest stocking dried mushrooms in the larder—they keep for a long time and can quickly be reconstituted to add their deep, earthy flavor to dishes. We use them here as an addition to our vinaigrette.

....

MAKES ABOUT 1¼ CUP/300 ML

1 cup/240 ml hot water
½ cup/15 grams dried porcini
　　mushrooms
2 tablespoons porcini-soaking
　　liquid (see below)
1 cup/240 ml Via Carota
　　Vinaigrette (page 340)
2 sprigs fresh marjoram

Pour water over porcini in a small bowl. Cover the bowl and steep until the mushrooms are soft, about 30 minutes. Drain through a fine-mesh strainer set over a bowl. Squeeze the liquid out of the mushrooms into the bowl, reserving 2 tablespoons. Finely chop the porcini and stir into the vinaigrette, with the porcini liquid. Pull the marjoram leaves off the stems, finely chop, and stir them into the vinaigrette.

Dried porcini vinaigrette can be refrigerated up to 3 days.

Salmoriglio

LEMON AND GARLIC DRESSING

Salmoriglio is an all-purpose summery dressing. We use it in several recipes throughout this book, as a marinade and as a vinaigrette.

....

MAKES ABOUT 1½ CUPS/360 ML

¼ cup + 2 tablespoons/90 ml
   lemon juice (from 2 lemons)
4 garlic cloves, finely grated
   (about 2 teaspoons)
1½ teaspoons/4.5 grams salt
½ teaspoon/1 gram chili flakes
1 teaspoon/3 grams dried oregano
1 tablespoon/15 ml water
¾ cup/180 ml extra-virgin olive oil
¼ cup/60 ml neutral oil such as
   safflower
a few sprigs fresh flat-leaf parsley,
   finely chopped

Combine the lemon juice, garlic, salt, chili flakes, oregano, and water in a small bowl. Slowly pour in the oils, whisking constantly. Stir in the parsley.

Stir briskly just before using; the lemon and garlic will have settled to the bottom. Salmoriglio is best used the day it's made, but will keep, refrigerated, for up to 3 days.

TIP · TO STEADY A BOWL

When making something like mayonnaise or vinaigrette by hand, you need one hand for whisking and the other for slowly pouring the oil, so it helps to have a steady bowl.

Here's how to prevent your bowl from skidding on the work surface: Place a dampened kitchen towel or two sheets of dampened paper towel flat on the counter and rest your bowl on it. Or roll the towel into a rope and make a nest on the counter in which you place the bowl. Now you can whisk away, using both hands. This also works to ensure that your cutting board is nonslip. Our cooks set up their workstation by sticking a damp towel under the cutting board before they start cooking.

TIP · TO FIX A BROKEN MAYONNAISE

Sometimes, while adding oil to egg yolk, the emulsification process fails. You will know because the two will separate and look curdled. Don't throw it away! To rebuild the mayonnaise, crack a new egg yolk into a clean bowl and whisk in a bit more oil, drop by drop, until it's holding together, with no visible oil particles. Then slowly and gradually whisk in the broken mayonnaise until it's all incorporated. Adjust the thickness with a few drops of water or lemon juice.

Aioli

GARLIC MAYONNAISE

A garlicky, traditional southern French mayonnaise is a staple at our table. Ours is not quite as intense as the traditional Provençal sauce because we use a whole egg rather than just the yolk. It lightens up the aioli in color and texture.

MAKES ABOUT 2 CUPS/
480 GRAMS

1 lemon

1 large egg, at room temperature

1 tablespoon/15 ml water

salt

½ cup/120 ml neutral oil such as safflower

1 cup/240 ml extra-virgin olive oil

1 garlic clove, finely grated

Finely zest the lemon into a medium bowl and add the egg, 1 teaspoon/5 ml lemon juice, 1 teaspoon/5 ml of water, and a pinch of salt. Pour in the safflower oil, drop by drop, whisking to incorporate each drop, until the mixture has emulsified (there should be no visible drops or streaks of oil), and is beginning to thicken.

When all the safflower oil has been incorporated, whisk in another teaspoon/ 5 ml of water, and slowly add the olive oil in a thin stream, whisking constantly as you pour, until all the oil has been incorporated in a creamy sauce. Stir in the garlic and remaining lemon juice, and add salt to taste.

If you would like the aioli to be thicker, add up to 2 tablespoons/30 ml more oil— either type will do. Aioli can sit at room temperature for up to 2 hours. After that it should be refrigerated. It will keep, covered in the refrigerator, for 2 days.

Salsa Verde

FRESH HERB AND CAPER SAUCE

MAKES ABOUT ½ CUP/120 ML

2 tablespoons/30 grams capers,
  rinsed and chopped
1 garlic clove, finely grated
1 lemon
salt
¼ cup/60 ml extra-virgin olive oil
  + more if needed
handful fresh flat-leaf parsley
  leaves (½ cup loosely packed
  leaves)
handful fresh basil leaves (½ cup
  loosely packed leaves)

Stir together the capers and garlic in a small bowl and squeeze in the juice of half the lemon, about ¼ teaspoon/1 gram salt, and the olive oil. Finely chop the parsley and add to the bowl. Stack the basil leaves on top of each other in an orderly way. Roll them up and draw your knife across them to make fine shreds. Coarsely chop the shreds, and add to the bowl.

Season the salsa verde with more salt and lemon juice as needed. Pour a thin layer of olive oil on top to prevent it from discoloring, if not using right away. Refrigerate for up to 1 day.

CHIFFONADE

There is a word for slicing fresh herb leaves into very thin ribbons, as we do here, and it's French: chiffonade. Yes, Rita is Italian, but she is more of a stickler for this technique than I am. Sometimes my chiffonade isn't fine enough because I'm distracted or in a hurry. In truth, I really just want to tear the leaves with my bare hands. But it's worth knowing how to do this so you can have thinly sliced herbs for your salad. **JODY**

BROTHS AND BRINES

In our cooking, we don't rely on poultry or meat
stocks very much. We like to let the flavors of each
ingredient shine, so we most often use water or a
simple vegetable broth when we're cooking risotto,
a ragù, or soup. Another recipe we rely on regularly
is court bouillon, which is a quick poaching liquid
for vegetables like artichokes and cardoons, and for
seafood. We brine all white meats before cooking
them to keep them moist and season them all the
way through.

Vegetable Broth

This is the template for our basic vegetable broth. We make large batches of this and add other vegetable trimmings and stems, depending on the season and what we have on hand. You should do the same, but avoid cruciferous vegetables such as cabbages and cauliflower, which will overpower the flavor, and potatoes, which will make the stock cloudy. Mushroom stems, fennel stalks, green garlic ends, and root vegetable peelings can be flavorful additions. If you add more vegetables, then you can increase the volume of water, too.

MAKES ABOUT 1½ QUARTS/
1½ LITERS

3 medium onions
6 medium carrots
5 celery stalks
3 quarts/3 liters cold water
**½ teaspoon/1–2 grams whole
  peppercorns**
**large handful fresh flat-leaf
  parsley, mostly stems**

Dice the onions, carrots, and celery into 1 inch/2.5 cm pieces. Combine them in a deep pot and pour in the water. Bring to a boil over high heat and skim off any foam that rises to the top. Reduce the heat to low and add the peppercorns and parsley. Simmer gently, partly covered, for 1½ hours.

Let the stock cool slightly before straining. Vegetable broth can be refrigerated for up to 2 days.

Court Bouillon

We use this light poaching liquid for many things, including artichokes (see Carciofi alla Griglia, page 19), cardoons (see Cardi Fritti, page 283), and seafood (see Insalata Frutti di Mare, page 104).

MAKES ABOUT 3 QUARTS/
3 LITERS

10 cups/2½ liters water
2½ cups/600 ml white wine
½ fennel bulb, or trimmings
3 celery stalks, cut in half
2 fresh or dried bay leaves
2 tablespoons/20 grams salt

Pour the water and wine into a large pot and add the fennel, celery, and bay leaves. Bring to a boil, then reduce the heat to medium-low. Stir in the salt and simmer, uncovered, for 20 minutes. Let cool slightly, then strain. Use right away or refrigerate for up to 1 week.

Brine

We make large batches of brine and add handfuls of whole herbs, and heads of garlic sliced crossways for maximum flavor. Taste it before you pour it over the meat you'll be brining—it should be less salty than the sea, with just enough sugar to balance it.

....

MAKES 2½ QUARTS/2½ LITERS

½ cup/75 grams salt
3 tablespoons/36 grams sugar
3 cups/720 ml boiling water
Whole black peppercorns
2 garlic heads, sliced in half
large handful fresh herb sprigs,
   such as rosemary and thyme
6 cups/1.5 liters cold water

Choose a container large enough to hold all 2½ quarts/2½ liters of brine plus the meat you'll be brining. Combine the salt and sugar in the container and pour boiling water over them; stir to dissolve. Add about 1 teaspoon/ 3 grams peppercorns, the garlic, and herbs, and pour the cold water into the container and stir. Cool to lukewarm before adding the meat.

....

TIP · BRINE

Brining meat is an extra step that helps lean white meat retain its juiciness when it's cooked. The salt in the brine also seasons the meat throughout, so this is an opportunity for adding other aromatics, such as fennel and coriander seeds, bay leaves, or juniper berries. Although brining could not be simpler, it does require planning ahead, which is second nature when you're a restaurant chef. At home just make sure there is space in your refrigerator for a container large enough to hold the meat and brine for two to three days.

Rigatina

CURED PORK BELLY

*We cure whole pork belly in
our house brine and then slice
it into triple-thick bacon at least
½ inch/1.3 cm thick.*

....

SERVES FOUR

¼ cup + 2 tablespoons/40 grams
    salt

3 tablespoons/36 grams sugar

6 cups/1.5 liters water

whole peppercorns

8 garlic cloves, crushed

4 sprigs fresh herbs, such as
    rosemary and thyme

2 pounds/1 kg boneless pork belly,
    in 1 piece

Make the brine: Combine salt and sugar with 2 cups/480 ml water in a small saucepan. Stir over low heat just to dissolve the salt and sugar. Add a few pinches of the peppercorns, and the garlic and herbs. Remove from the heat and stir in the remaining water. Set aside to cool until lukewarm.

If the pork belly has skin on one side, slice off the skin carefully with a long, sharp knife; hold the blade flat against the pork to shave off the outer layer. Place the pork belly in a straight-sided container deep and large enough to hold it and all the brine, about 9 x 13 inches/23 x 33 cm and at least 2 to 3 inches/5 to 7.5 cm deep. Add the brine and make sure the belly is completely submerged. Refrigerate for 2 or 3 days; after 2 days the pork will be mildly salty with a soft texture, and after 3 days it will be firmer.

Remove pork from the brine and pat dry. Keep it refrigerated until ready to cook, up to 2 days. Before cooking, slice lengthwise into thick strips (1 to 1½ inches/2.5 to 4 cm).

CONSERVES AND SEASONINGS

These are some of the things we prepare long before the orders come in from the dining room, and we keep them on hand for amplifying the flavors of a dish. Like batches of freshly toasted fennel seed salt, a seasoned pork fat mixture, and slow-cooked garlic cloves in olive oil.

TIP · STERILIZING JARS

Sterilize your jars just before you begin; when working with hot food, the jars should still be hot so you can put the prepared food directly into them.

First, wash the jars and their lids thoroughly with hot, soapy water. Then, place the jars upright on a rack inside a large pot, and add enough hot water to completely submerge the jars. Bring to a boil, cover the pot, and boil for 10 minutes. (It is not necessary to sterilize the lids.) Shake out the water and set the jars on a clean dish towel to dry. Fill the jars and screw on the lids while still hot.

Strutto

SEASONED PORK FAT

Use this to season pork chops when making Braciole al Latte (page 242).

....
MAKES ABOUT 1 CUP/230 GRAMS

4 ounces/115 grams pancetta,
   in thick slices
4 ounces/115 grams trimmed pork
   fat or fresh pork belly
2 large garlic cloves
2 sprigs fresh rosemary
1 teaspoon/3 grams Fennel Seed
   Salt (page 357) + more for
   seasoning chops

Cube the pancetta and mix it with the pork fat. Chop with a sharp chef's knife, or pulse in a food processor until ground into a coarse paste. Finely chop the garlic and the rosemary leaves (or pulse in the machine) and add to the mixture; stir in the fennel seed salt. Transfer to sterilized jars (see instructions on page 000). Strutto can be made ahead and refrigerated for up to 1 week.

Garlic Confit

Sizzle cloves of garlic in the pan alongside the Svizzerina (page 305) or nestle the cloves among layers of our Cardi Fritti (page 283).

....

FOR 2 HEADS OF GARLIC

**2 plump heads of garlic,
about 24 large cloves**

2 small sprigs fresh rosemary

**extra-virgin olive oil, up to
about 1 cup/240 ml**

Separate the garlic cloves, leaving their skins intact. Place the garlic with rosemary in a very small pot and cover completely with olive oil (about ¾ cup/180 ml). Set the pot over the lowest possible heat and cook until garlic cloves are completely soft when pressed with a fork, about 45 minutes. Check to maintain a very low heat—a few small bubbles are fine but don't let the oil simmer. Cool the garlic in its oil, then transfer the garlic and oil to a sterilized jar (see instructions, page 000) and refrigerate, submerged in the oil, for up to 2 weeks.

GARLIC CONFIT

Slow-cooking olive oil and other fats = tenderness. Our garlic confit is really short-term conserving; we make big batches of it and refrigerate it for two weeks or until we use it all up. The Tonno Sott'Olio (page 356) is also a refrigerated pantry item. We mash it into butter for crostini (page 311), in tramezzini sandwiches for the bar (page 186), and in salads, see Fagioli e Tonno (page 138).

Tonno Sott'olio

OLIVE OIL–PRESERVED TUNA

When local albacore tuna is plentiful, the odds and ends are well suited for this quick and flavorful sott'olio.

. . . .

SERVES FOUR TO SIX

1 pound/454 grams fresh albacore
    tuna pieces, sliced about 1 inch/
    2.5 cm thick
salt
peel of half a lemon
2 garlic cloves, lightly crushed
about 10 whole peppercorns
1 dried red chili
3 sprigs fresh thyme
extra-virgin olive oil

Sprinkle the tuna lightly with salt and toss to coat evenly, let stand for 30 minutes. Put the lemon peel, garlic, peppercorns, chili, and thyme in a small saucepan; place tuna pieces snugly on top and pour in enough oil to completely submerge it (about 1½–2 cups/360–480 ml depending on size of the pot).

Warm the tuna over the lowest possible heat just until it's opaque, 10 to 15 minutes—you may see a few small bubbles rise up from the bottom of the pot, but don't let the oil come to a simmer. Lift tuna out of the oil with a slotted spoon, and pack into one or two sterilized jars until about two thirds full (see instructions for sterilizing jars, page 352). Strain the olive oil through a sieve into the jars, submerging the tuna completely. Cover tightly. Set the jars on a cooling rack for 30 minutes before refrigerating. Tonno sott'olio can be refrigerated for about one week.

Each time you remove a piece of tuna, make sure the remaining pieces are covered by olive oil.

Fennel Seed Salt

A seasoned salt is a nice finishing touch for grilled mushrooms (like those on page 194), and it suits most pork dishes (see Braciole al Latte, page 242). It's a simple ratio of 1:2. Keep that formula in mind and use it to make seasoned salts with other spices in your cabinet.

Lightly toast the fennel seeds in a dry skillet over medium heat, tossing occasionally until fragrant and golden, about 2 minutes. Pour onto a plate to cool. Combine with the salt in a mortar, and pound with a pestle until finely ground, or use a spice grinder. Store in an airtight jar away from heat and direct light; it will keep for about 2 weeks.

1 teaspoon/3 grams of fennel seeds
   or other whole-seed spice
2 teaspoons/6 grams salt

Ricotta Affumicata

SMOKED RICOTTA

We use smoked ricotta as a filling for our Tortelli di Ricotta Affumicata (page 214), and we suggest spreading it on crostini with Confettura di Cipolla (page 217) or sliced, grilled vegetables. It is a product unique to southern Italy and can be hard to find, even there. Luckily for us, a small producer named Salvatore Brooklyn makes and sells excellent smoked ricotta in New York. Here is a recipe for making your own smoked ricotta on a charcoal grill. Of course, if you aren't up for the project, you can use plain ricotta instead. This is a cold-smoking process; the temperature is kept cool by nestling the cheese in ice while it's being smoked.

MAKES 1 POUND/454 GRAMS,
SERVES 6

1½ pounds/680 grams fresh ricotta cheese
　　at room temperature
enough ice to half-fill a 9 x 13 inch/23 x 33 cm
　　baking pan

EQUIPMENT YOU WILL NEED

cheesecloth and string for tying
6 hardwood charcoal briquettes (do not
　　use coal soaked with lighter fluid)
2 handfuls woodchips for smoking
1 aluminum pie pan (8 inches/20 cm)
1 straight-sided aluminum baking pan
　　(9 x 13 inches/23 x 33 cm)
salt

Wrap the ricotta in a double layer of cheesecloth or set it in a fine-mesh strainer over a bowl to drain. Refrigerate until the ricotta has released all its water (3 to 4 tablespoons/45 to 60 ml), about 1 hour.

Light the charcoal briquettes (ideally in a chimney starter) and dump them on the lower grate of a charcoal grill, off to one side. Sprinkle a handful of woodchips evenly over the charcoal. Cover the grill with a lid, keeping the vents open. Wait for smoke to begin pouring out of the vents.

Meanwhile, spoon the ricotta into the aluminum pie pan. Fill the large baking pan halfway with ice and nestle the pan of ricotta into the ice. Open the grill and place the pan of ice with ricotta in it on the upper grate of the grill. Close the lid.

Open the grill every 5 minutes to stir the ricotta. The smoky flavor will permeate the ricotta gradually—begin tasting after 10 minutes and take the ricotta off the grill after about 15 minutes (or when it's as smoky as you like it). The smokiness will mellow overnight. Season to taste with salt. Refrigerate smoked ricotta up to 3 days.

PASTA AND DOUGHS

At the core of the daily routine at Via Carota is the making of doughs. We have one egg pasta (Pasta Sfoglia) for tagliatelle and folded shapes, and a semolina dough (Pasta di Semola) that has enough structure to be used for hand-rolled pasta and lasagna sheets.

When it comes to pastry, we use the same dough for all our tarts, and we stick to a few, trusted recipes. And rather than hire a pastry chef we are lucky to have cooks who put their heart and soul into making our desserts.

Pasta Sfoglia

FRESH EGG PASTA

We use this dough to make
Stracci con Pesto di Fave
(page 11), Tagliatelle al Tartufo
(page 323), and Tortelli di
Ricotta Affumicata (page 359);
see individual recipes for rolling
and cutting specifications.

....

MAKES 12 OUNCES/340 GRAMS,
SERVES FOUR

1⅔ cups/200 grams type 00 flour
   + more for the work surface
½ teaspoon/1.5 grams salt
2 large eggs, lightly beaten
1 tablespoon + 1 teaspoon/20 ml
   extra-virgin olive oil
2–3 tablespoons/30–45 ml water

TO MIX BY HAND Whisk the flour and salt together in a bowl, then pour onto a work surface in a mound. Make a deep well in the center of the flour with a fork. Add the eggs and olive oil to the center of the well and whisk them together. Use the fork or your fingers to gradually incorporate flour from the inside walls into the eggs, mixing from the bottom first. Gather the flour and egg into a shaggy dough using a bench scraper and your hands, picking up any loose flour. Add water as needed until it all comes together. Pat into a firm dough and scrape the work surface clean.

Lightly dust the surface with flour and work the dough, kneading and folding it into a ball. Continue kneading until the dough is smooth and soft, about 10 minutes. Slightly flatten the ball of dough and place a bowl over it, or wrap it tightly in plastic wrap.

Rest the dough for 30 minutes and up to 24 hours before rolling and cutting. Refrigerate if resting for more than 2 hours.

IN A MIXER The dough can easily be made in a food processor or a stand mixer. Combine the dry ingredients and, with the machine running, pour in the wet ingredients while pulsing or mixing just until it all comes together. Turn the dough out onto a work surface, gather any crumbly flour, and knead by hand—or switch to a dough hook attachment. Knead until the dough is smooth and soft. Slightly flatten the ball of dough and wrap it tightly in plastic wrap.

Pasta di Semola

SEMOLINA FLOUR PASTA

Use this dough to make Trofie (page 130) and Pici (page 238). A double batch of this recipe makes enough pasta for our ten-layer Lasagna Cacio e Pepe (page 299). Semolina dough can require a longer kneading time than fresh egg pasta does. If it still feels firm after kneading, trust that the dough will hydrate and soften as it rests.

....

MAKES 14 OUNCES/400 GRAMS,
SERVES FOUR

1 cup/116 grams type 00 flour

1 cup/150 grams semolina

salt

2 tablespoons/30 ml extra-virgin
    olive oil

½ cup plus 2 tablespoons/150 ml
    water

TO MIX BY HAND Whisk the flour, semolina, and a large pinch of salt together in a bowl, then pour onto a work surface in a mound. Make a deep well in the center of the flour with a fork. Add the olive oil and about ¼ cup/60 ml water. Use the fork or your fingers to gradually incorporate flour from the inside of the well, mixing from the bottom first in a circular motion. Pour in the remaining water, and gather the mixture into a shaggy dough using a bench scraper and your hands. Pat into a firm dough and scrape the work surface clean.

Work the dough vigorously, kneading and folding it into a ball. Continue kneading until the dough is smooth and elastic, 10–15 minutes. Slightly flatten the ball of dough and place a bowl over it, or wrap it tightly in plastic wrap.

Rest the dough for 1 hour and up to 24 hours before rolling and cutting.

IN A MIXER The dough can easily be made in a food processor or a stand mixer. Combine the dry ingredients and, with the machine running, pour in the wet ingredients while pulsing or mixing just until it all comes together. Turn the dough out onto a work surface, gather any crumbly flour, and knead by hand—or switch to a dough hook attachment to knead in the machine. Knead until the dough is smooth and elastic. Slightly flatten the ball of dough and place a bowl over it, or wrap it tightly in plastic wrap.

Semolina Flour Pasta for Lasagna

This is a double batch of the Pasta di Semola recipe, enough to make one pan of lasagna.

MAKES 28 OUNCES/800 GRAMS, SERVES EIGHT

2 cups/232 grams type oo flour

2 cups/320 grams semolina

salt

4 tablespoons/60 ml extra-virgin olive oil

1¼ cup/300 ml water

TO MIX BY HAND Whisk the flour, semolina, and a couple of pinches of salt together in a bowl, then pour onto a work surface in a mound. Make a deep well in the center of the flour with a fork. Add the olive oil and about ½ cup/120 ml water. Use the fork or your fingers to gradually incorporate flour from the inside of the well, mixing from the bottom in a circular motion. Pour in the remaining water, and gather the mixture into a shaggy dough using a bench scraper and your hands. Pat into a firm dough and scrape the work surface clean.

Work the dough vigorously, kneading and folding it into a ball. Continue kneading until the dough is smooth and elastic, 10–15 minutes. Slightly flatten the ball of dough and place a bowl over it, or wrap it tightly in plastic wrap.

Rest the dough for 1 hour and up to 24 hours before rolling and cutting.

IN A MIXER The dough can easily be made in a food processor or a stand mixer. Combine the dry ingredients and, with the machine running, pour in the wet ingredients while pulsing or mixing just until it all comes together. Turn the dough out onto a work surface, gather any crumbly flour, and knead by hand—or switch to a dough hook attachment. Knead until the dough is smooth and elastic. Slightly flatten the ball of dough and place a bowl over it, or wrap it tightly in plastic wrap.

Pasta Frolla

SWEET PASTRY DOUGH

This dough is buttery and enriched with egg yolks; it makes a tender and flavorful crostata shell. We give instructions for making the dough in the food processor because it's the quickest and most fail-proof method. Of course, making pastry without a machine is enjoyable, so if you are nimble with your fingers, go ahead—the steps are the basically the same. Chill the dough well and work quickly while rolling it. Don't worry about perfection; we do lots of patching in the pan, pressing any broken pieces back together.

MAKES 2 CROSTATE OR
1 CROSTATA WITH A LATTICE TOP

2 cups/240 grams all-purpose
   flour
½ cup/100 grams sugar
¼ teaspoon/.75 gram salt
2 sticks/225 grams cold unsalted
   butter, thinly sliced
finely grated zest of half an orange
   (about 1 teaspoon)
2 large egg yolks, lightly beaten

Combine the flour, sugar, and salt in the bowl of a food processor and pulse to blend them. Add the butter and pulse a few times until the mixture is crumbly with a few almond-sized pieces of butter.

Add the orange zest and, with the machine running, pour the egg yolks through the feed tube into the dough. Pulse just until the dough comes together against the sides of the bowl. Turn the dough onto a work surface. Gather any flour, press the dough until compact, and knead lightly a couple of times. If making the dough by hand, whisk the dry ingredients together in a bowl and rub in the butter with your fingertips until barely crumbly with a few almond-sized pieces, then stir in the zest and egg yolks.

Divide the dough into two pieces, and tightly wrap each piece in parchment paper or plastic wrap. Press into disks (about ¾ inch/ 2 cm thick). Refrigerate for at least 1 hour before rolling, up to 2 days. Pasta frolla can be frozen for 1 month.

Acknowledgments

We thank the team at Knopf and our agent Janis Donnaud for connecting all the dots and believing in the beauty of Via Carota. Many thanks and much appreciation for our dear collaborator, the gifted Anna Kovel, who brought our story to life and worked to develop these recipes that home cooks can embrace, with support in recipe testing from Shira Bocar, and conversions, both metric and linguistic, from Natalie Danford.

Thanks to Louise Fili for her beautiful graphics. Thanks also to the brilliant photographers Andrea Gentl, Marty Hyers, and their support Lucia Bell-Epstein, Sahara Ndiaye, as well as Rebecca Jurkevich and stylist Ayesha Patel, who elegantly captured the spirit of Via Carota season by season.

We are enormously grateful to the hard-working people on our staff, especially our extraordinary family of cooks at Via Carota, whose dedication and care for each other honor their craft and make everything truly possible and delicious. They are inspiring, as are all our vital producers, makers, and growers who cultivate the earth far and near.

To Sheik MD Shohidul Islam, our kind and thoughtful leader, who looks after all of us on Grove Street. Thank you Claudia Bellini for your support on all fronts; and cherished friend and mentor Kathy Kranhold.

Rita and I are blessed to live and work in the West Village. Thank you to this community for all the love and support you share. And finally, we thank all the kind and patient guests who make our home at Via Carota theirs.

Index

Page numbers in *italics* refer to illustrations.

A NOTE ABOUT THE AUTHORS

Jody Williams and Rita Sodi opened the much-acclaimed
Via Carota in the West Village in 2014. They have cooked
and collaborated together for more than a decade. *The New
York Times* described them as "one of the great partnerships
in the New York restaurant scene." In 2019, Jody and Rita,
two self-taught chefs, were awarded the James Beard Award
for Best Chef in New York City for Via Carota. They opened
Bar Pisellino, a celebration of the Italian bar, across the
street from Via Carota in 2019. Jody and Rita established
the Shaker-inspired Commerce Inn in 2021. Rita is also the
chef and owner of the perennial favorite I Sodi, part of the
fabric of the West Village. Jody is the chef and founder of
the beloved Buvette, just down the street from Via Carota;
Buvette is also in Paris, Tokyo, London, and Mexico City.
The couple married in 2015 at New York City Hall.

A NOTE ON THE TYPE

This book was set in Legacy Serif. Ronald Arnholm (b. 1939) designed the Legacy family after being inspired by the 1470 edition of *Eusebius* set in the roman type of Nicolas Jenson. This revival type maintains much of the character of the original. Its serifs, stroke weights, and varying curves give Legacy Serif its distinct appearance. It was released by the International Typeface Corporation in 1992.

Composed by North Market Street Graphics,
Lancaster, Pennsylvania

Printed and bound by C&C Offset,
China

Book design by Pei Loi Koay

JODY WILLIAMS is the chef and owner
of the much acclaimed Buvette in the West
Village and co-chef/owner with Rita Sodi
of Via Carota, an Italian restaurant the
couple opened in 2014. Williams is also the
author of *Buvette: The Pleasure of Good Food*.

RITA SODI is the chef and owner of the ever-
popular I Sodi and co-chef/owner with Jody
Williams of Via Carota, the restaurant that is
inspired by her seventeenth-century country
house in the hills near Florence. Commerce
Inn is the couple's latest restaurant
collaboration.

viacarota.com
Twitter, Facebook, and Instagram: @viacarota

Cover photograph by Gentl & Hyers
Cover design by John Gall

ALFRED A. KNOPF, PUBLISHER, NEW YORK
aaknopf.com
9/2022